Beyond the
Broken Church

Beyond the
Broken
Church

How to Leave Church
Problems Behind Without
Leaving the Church

Previously titled *Dear Church*

Sarah Cunningham

 ZONDERVAN®

ZONDERVAN

Beyond the Broken Church
Copyright © 2006, 2014 by Sarah Raymond Cunningham

Previously published as *Dear Church*

This title is also available as a Zondervan ebook.
Visit www.zondervan.com/ebooks.

Requests for information should be addressed to:

Zondervan, 3900 *Sparks Dr., Grand Rapids, Michigan 49546*

This edition: ISBN 978-0-310-33694-5 (Softcover)

Library of Congress Cataloging-in-Publication Data

Cunningham, Sarah.
        Dear church: letters from a disillusioned generation / Sarah Cunningham.
            p.   cm.
        Includes bibliographical references.
        ISBN 978-0-310-26958-8
        1. Church controversies. 2. Generation X — Religious life.
        3. Generation Y — Religious life. I. Title.
        BV652.9.C86 2006
        262 — dc22   2005037177

Cover design: Kirk DouPonce/Dog Eared Design
Cover photography: iStockphoto
Interior design: Katherine Lloyd, The DESK

Printed in the United States of America

14 15 16 17 18 19 20 /DCI/ 20 19 18 17 16 15 14 13 12 11 10 9 8 7 6 5 4 3 2 1

To all those who've been exhausted by church,
who've been worn out, gossiped about,
and run dry.
For those who've experienced oppression at her hand,
who've seen her power abused,
and shed tears in her wake.
For those inside and outside the church's walls,
who've heaved upon her their hopes and dreams,
and who sit on the sidelines or look on from a distance,
feeling, at least at times, disappointed and abandoned.
This book is for you.

Contents

Preface:
This Is Important

Dear Readers,

This is not a book about being disillusioned. It's a book about moving beyond it.

Like many of you, I used to fiercely believe the church was the most powerful source of hope on the planet. Then I grew up, or should I say, grew up *further* and stumbled into that painful, expanded awareness that sometimes comes with adulthood. There I encountered a lengthy list of religious flaws and a side of the church that appeared far from hopeful.

Unfortunately, I was not the only one. So many young adults have left their pews in search of escape, or maybe in search of a better way, that we quickly have become the focus of in-depth studies on religious trends. A multigenerational group of exhausted, depleted, and often jaded former church attendees can be seen wandering in the cloudy landscape just outside the church's doors.

Almost everyone, it seems, has a story to tell about some painful or disastrous encounter with the church. And that ache manifests itself in different ways. Some abandon the church scene to run for what they deem more gracious or authentic hills, while others quietly swallow weekly helpings of resentment from the front row or even from the stage of the church sanctuary.

However you manage your frustrations, this book is for you. It's for those of you who have walked through dark stages of disillusionment in the past, it's for those of you who are disenchanted with church right this minute, and it's for those of you who haven't hit the hard stuff yet but are just wise enough to suspect imperfect days lie ahead.

The chapters ahead may also be a starting point for those seeking to better understand a son or daughter, family friend, or former youth group member who grew up in church only to disappear from the pews altogether. And the appendices contain extensive resources that provide insights for church and denominational leaders for those of you who have been caught off guard by the gradual exodus of the young and now worriedly wonder about the future of your graying congregations.

You are all welcome and needed to make this ongoing conversation a healthy one. I hold on to hope that together we will find the best next steps in sifting our reality, as a church who must move beyond our imperfect moments to bear hope to the world.

You, like me, have likely surrendered to the idea that as long as humankind lives in freedom, we will experience suffering. Similarly, I suspect as long as we have convictions about our faith, we will also have disillusionment. I hope, though, that as long as we have disillusionment, we will fight toward better days together.

Headed toward fullness,
Sarah

Introduction:
Read This First

Books that promise to delve into disillusionment with organized religion raise suspicion. Rightly so.

I wouldn't expect those of you who are worn down by church to eagerly believe these pages will somehow retroactively correct the injustice in your faith story or instantly soothe the wounds you've incurred. Your disillusionment is complex, layered, and shaped by your story and particular events unique to you.

A book can't penetrate all the details of your journey, nor can it single-handedly heal your religious injuries. Unfortunately, there is no simple, overnight formula for righting your journey. I can only offer the ideas and actions that eventually created breathing room for me, that pushed out the institutional walls closing in on me and gave me space to feel whole and connected again. I hope you'll find that some of the things that prompted me toward well-being are not only worthwhile to my story but hold value for you as well.

To those of you serving in the church, I also understand why you may be hesitant about the title *Beyond the Broken Church*. You are committed to the mission of Christ and your local church, and you may feel defensive about those who take aim at the good faith work going on in your community. And rightly so.

You *will* find some cynicism here, and it may be hard to absorb. These honest, sometimes angst-filled, even sometimes immature feelings represent a hard and vulnerable time in my spiritual development. And while I was tempted to delete or polish some of the frustrations I voiced before they were preserved in this book, to try to present a more refined or sophisticated version of myself, I've decided to leave most of the original tone intact.

The truth is I've walked through some tragic church-related events. It hasn't been easy. And I sometimes vented in ways that I would later consider over the top. But the emotions of that stage were real, and allowing them to grace these pages in all their messy glory makes me a more relatable friend to those moving through disillusionment.

I hope you can see, as you read, that it is not my aim to bash the church. I could never take a stab at the church without drawing blood from my own skin, because church is a deep and sacred part of my identity.

If you read the book through to the end, I think you'll actually find I'm a familiar face — the archetype of many cowlicked and pigtailed children who grew up performing Christmas plays or belting out songs with exaggerated motions in your Sunday school classes and sanctuaries. Consider, for example, the two excerpts from my books below. My guess is you'll find pieces of yourself or those you love in my story.

Sundays were noticeably elevated from the rest of my week. They were mysterious, sensuous, full of ambience. The wooden pews, whose ends curled into elegant swirls of carved wood, smelled faintly of Murphy's oil soap as they cushioned me in deep teal fabric. I felt enthroned on them. Postured for something important.

My foot would rock methodically as live music swelled to fill the sanctuary, sending drumbeats and vocal riffs floating to the glossy knotted pine rafters. My fingers traced the goose-bumped cover and translucent, tissue-thin pages of ancient Scripture. The rows of black and sometimes red print held story and wisdom worthy of its gold-rimmed pages. Even to a child, the reading was hearty and satisfying. An indulgence as sweet as chocolate and as filling as a Sunday roast.

By some great feat of architecture, even the church building itself seemed enchanted, as if positioned to pull in the high noon sun. And so just before the invitational hymn drew the audience to their feet, loose streams of sun would pierce the colored windows, painting a kalei-doscope of reflections onto the floor and walls.

The carpeted aisles people solemnly walked during altar calls were also known to hum with a sort of electric, person-to-person warmth as well. This collective charm was robust and nourishing, the type that resulted only when you gath-ered a familiar community from vantage points around the city to some pew or foyer or other holy meeting ground.

And in some rare moments, I remember, the room fell into a beautiful silence, as if some faint and sacred voice was whispering to everyone in attendance, entreating us to listen carefully. Taking us gently by the chins and lulling our minds into reflection and solitude.

It was a holy shushing.[1]

During worship, I knew which drumbeat to clap to and I knew when to belt out the lyrics in passionate allegiance with those around me and when to whisper the words softly so as not to interrupt the quiet, reflective atmosphere the music leader was attempting. I knew when to close my eyes and exactly what angle to bow my head in order to give off the expected amount of reverence during corporate prayer. I knew when to open my eyes and when to nod; when to pick up my pen and use it to take "notes" to convey I was listening intently.

I had the churchy social graces in the bag as well. I knew when to lean into a boisterous hug from a suit-clad usher and I knew how to tilt my head to minimize the damage when little old ladies smeared me with lipstick. I shook hands and set up chairs and passed out cloth-covered teal hymnbooks — one every other seat.

I knew where to find anything you wanted: mops, Kool-Aid mix, or the tiny plastic communion cups that never hold enough grape juice. And I knew where everything belonged: what to do with used bulletins, where to stack excess chairs, and which families should receive the wrapped potluck leftovers that may or may not have been a blessing — depending on how much gravy was involved in any given recipe. If the church world had a Carmen Sandiego game show equivalent, where kids ran all over the map putting things in the right place, I would've been the champion.[2]

As you can see based on my experiences, I can write genuinely about love *and* disillusionment in the same breath because, like many of you and those you love, my faith has had both wholesome and dysfunctional moments, stretches where I've heartily celebrated faith communities and stretches where I've smacked into disheartening sides of the church I never wanted to discover.

Perhaps many of you can relate because church has given you a mix of rich and satisfying and difficult and troubling experiences as well.

And maybe, like me, you do not want to feel the way you do. Your disillusionment, like mine, may not be just some casual cynicism over religious cosmetics — over some congregation clinging to outdated songs or serving some less-than-hipster brand of coffee. You too may have witnessed events that left some local congregations wounded, derailing people's impressions of God and grace, scattering and dividing those who were once teamed in mission, and permanently scarring adults and children alike.

If you are disillusioned, then I invite you to join me in exploring the experiences that jaded you toward the church. I hope you will be inspired to sift through the feelings surrounding your frustrations, identify any bitterness that can be released, and gain some skills and perspective for dealing with future disappointments. And I hope you will join me in opening the communication lines that will provide space for new ideas and priorities in the church of tomorrow.

Moreover, I hope you, like me, will be able to salvage some of your energy and interest in faith community. Because despite the tensions and letdowns along my spiritual journey, there is no tension I'd rather engage, no cause I'd rather expend my energy on. More than anything else on the planet, I want to continue to shift more of my allegiance to Christ, to invite my fellow citizens to move beyond pain to experience the goodness and wholesomeness attached to Jesus' way of living.

Resolving my feelings about faith and church has not always been easy. In forcing myself to bring my own concerns and the resulting learnings to the surface, I have had to dig for the maturity and wisdom to face my own questions, examine my own flaws, and review my own position before God and others. With every passing year, I have to adjust for increasing awareness and growth. However, this passage beyond disillusionment has been a priceless journey for me, and as a result, it is a journey I wish for every one of you.

Some who pick up this book, I realize, will not be disillusioned. If you are a church leader who is currently enjoying a healthy stretch of church life, I hope you will benefit from such a raw telling of how disillusionment has affected me and others in our time. I hope you will hear in my story things people might be hesitant to say to you in person. And I hope you will be encouraged to help my peers and others examine their disillusionment so they can experience more of the fullness that comes with living Christ's ideals.

Regardless of where you are in your own journey or how you devote yourself in service to the church, odds are, at some point, you once held the ideal that the church could change the world. And, on many occasions, you struggled and perhaps still struggle — just as I and others do — against the idea that it so regularly fails.

Whether you are disillusioned or not, I am hoping that you will do more than just read these chapters, that you will find a way to engage them, perhaps by working through the included discussion questions by yourself or with a small group or by connecting with me online at my website (www.sarahcunningham.org), Facebook page (http://www.facebook.com/sarahcunninghampage), or Twitter profile (@sarahcunning). You can also add quotes or your own ideas to the discussion on Facebook or Twitter using the hashtag #brokenchurch.

Most of all, I am hoping that if you find common ground with me in church-related disappointments, you will also find common ground in my will to never give up. My prayer is that we can find ways to breathe new life into both our local churches and the global community of people who follow Christ.

Chapter 1

You Are
Not Alone

Y ou are not alone.

I've agonized over how to begin this conversation with those of you who, like me, know what it is to be wounded and grieved and dried up by religion. And these are the few words I've come to believe are most important for the occasion: *You are not alone.*

Before getting to this though, I should first acknowledge what a complex task it is to respond well to another's pains about church and faith. So many disappointments and emotions are in play, so many particulars that cannot be remedied by any single statement.

Nevertheless, there always seems to be some imprudent sap who replies to life-sidelining spiritual angst with oversimplified or patronizing remarks. He heroically pulls a pin from a lonely Scripture verse he's cut from the Bible and launches it like an enlightenment grenade onto the wounded.

Anguish over faith seems to unlock secret arsenals of cheesy religious slogans that some people of faith access, sincerely believing they will be helpful and life-giving, reminding the pained of some handy bit like the FROG acronym. When attached to a cartoon amphibian, they hope this reminder to *Fully Rely On God* will be the life raft that keeps us afloat in the darkest moments of life and faith. But despite the good intentions of these people, in matters of dishonesty, fraud, abuse of power, failed leadership, exclusion, broken marriages, judgment, or church splits, I am not convinced that bookmarks or wristbands are among the most helpful resources for healing.

I once spoke at a brunch for church leaders at an Arizona coffee shop. There I was asked a pointed question: *If you could gather all the religiously disillusioned into a stadium, and you could only speak to them for a few minutes, what would you say?*

I knew right away I had longed for the same kind of answers the questioner was seeking. That I too had hoped there might be some grand, singular solution — an antidote to spiritual sickness that could be administered the same way our culture uses antibiotics. *Swallow the meds. You'll start to feel better in the next twenty-four hours.*

The question of course is optimistic and perhaps misinformed from the start, as it is not helpful to suppose the answer lies in steering the disillusioned in masses, spraying them all with antiseptic like infected cattle. The hurting deserve their own individual, localized hearings. And to be helpful, the responses must deeply consider each person's unique makeup and circumstances.

As long as we're inviting hypotheticals, instead of gathering the world's disillusioned into a stadium, I wish that I could invite the disheartened, one by one, into some eclectic spiritual grandmother's house. That as she dusted various ceramic bears and commemorative coins and whipped up some fruit Jell-O concoction, she could listen in the way only veterans of the faith can. Brimming with sacredness and some sort of enduring okay-ness, she could take in everything the disillusioned want to say without being shocked or threatened.

This soulful grandmother would never break eye contact. Instead, she would hold all the expressed frustrations and hurts with her eyes, symbolically indicating by the coffee and Pepperidge Farm cookies she serves that she receives all the critique and yet still offers belonging. She would communicate, maybe through some silent nodding and gentle pats to the arm, that she has seen and heard these things before and that the hurting ones and their experiences are altogether normal.

This is much more the scenario in which I'd like you to hear the words we begin with: *You are not alone.*

In this spirit, I take up the task of writing to you about religious disaffection. I know the topic is surrounded by land mines, where even well-intentioned conversations accidentally stumble onto things that exacerbate pain instead of alleviate it. And there is always the possibility that a profound insight for one person will fall flat and seem roll-your-eyes ridiculous for someone else.

Yet I also know — deep in my bones — that saying nothing when someone's faith has been derailed by a bad religious experience is equally neglectful and irresponsible. So I ask for your grace as we begin to poke and prod at our discouragement. My ideas and your experiences are sure to rub against each other's hurts at times as we strike out to find or rediscover some stable footholds together. As we wade into these charged waters, it would be helpful for all of us to bulk up on generosity and benefit of the doubt.

I'll say it again: Take hope. *You are not alone.*

I'm sure you're not alone, for starters, because I am right here with you. I too have walked through stages where I got sick on bad religion. Born a PK (i.e., a pastor's kid, not a Promise Keeper), I logged hundreds of hours in the pews before I ever learned to pronounce the word *church*.

While some parents struggled to get their kids to take ownership in the local church, my parents faced a different challenge. Not only did I take ownership in our local church's mission, but I seemed to think I literally *owned* the building. I would have bet my offering that my signature was on the church deed, scribbled with the same visitor pen I used to play tic-tac-toe on the back of bulletins.

In fact, I probably still owe a few apologies to the many well-meaning adults who occasionally reminded me not to run in the church hallways. As I sped by, unaffected by their warnings, I would flash them the "Obviously you don't realize who you're talking to" look. *These are my hallways.*

As a pastor's kid, I took my role in the local church very seriously. Among a long list of other self-appointed responsibilities, I was in charge of flashing my dad a handwritten "It's 12:05!" sign when a particularly long sermon didn't seem to be coming in for a landing.

In short, my childhood was an eighteen-year course on Christian leadership. And while I like to joke about having front-row seats to seven days of sermons a week, I would not trade my initiation to the church for anything.

By the time I graduated from high school, I was on track to carry out Christ's mission with what was probably atypical intensity. I immediately gravitated toward Spring Arbor University, a Christian school in south-central Michigan that provided the perfect context for experimenting with my evolving ministry ideas. I doubt anyone was surprised four years later when, before I even received my degree, I launched my adult career as a full-time staffer at a local church.

And not just any local church. The first church I participated in as an adult was hands-down the most compelling context I'd ever seen the word *church* attached to. The attendees were passionate, the services were creative, the staff was driven. Community and passion were running on all six cylinders. And more than once I left our meetings so energized to think about Christ's mission that I missed my road while driving home. I was sure I was in the right place at the right time with the right people.

I can only hope all of you have experienced such striking highs in your own church experience.

Of course, like many of you, I also sometimes encountered headlines about tragedies that had befallen unknown churches elsewhere: church splits, financial fraud, pornography, child molestations, broken families, and so on. But I had the luxury of detachment, and so I needed only to muster a bit of short-lived sympathy before forgetting the plight of these unknown and usually distant communities.

In regard to my own church experiences, my adult years seemed to pick up right where my childhood left off: I was living, breathing, and bleeding church and having the time of my life doing it. And the more time I invested in the local church, the more I believed — I mean *really seriously believed* — that "the church is the hope of the world."

Of course, as the veterans among you can probably guess, my lifetime of church-related euphoria did not continue unchallenged. Somewhere in my early twenties, a series of disappointing life events crashed head-on into my growing awareness of Christianity's sometimes blemished historical track record. The personal fallout was ugly, and much of what I believed about church came crashing down around me.

I was surprised and disoriented as I watched comrades, church staff and volunteer leaders and attendees, seemingly rushing to break ranks with each other. I couldn't understand why the glue of faith that had once bonded us so tightly had dissolved just as quickly or why the beliefs we ascribed to didn't bring us to more perfect resolution. And mostly I couldn't fathom how pain and judgment, pride and division — including my own — could spew from communities that exist in the name of God. I felt immobilized and inept, like a young child who lacked the coping skills to sift through parental infighting or complete my own rite of passage.

The worst realization was a simple one. It gradually dawned on me that I could no longer invite to the same baby shower or Christmas party people who had once, in a kindred spirit, championed the same mission. Not comfortably anyway. And something about this reality, combined with my budding awareness of Christianity's historic evils, branded the concept of church a failure and blew my feelings about institutions wide open.

After all those years of running up and down church halls, weaving in and out of adult legs in its lobby, playing freeze tag on its lawn, and chilling with its people at potlucks and picnics, I was disappointed in the notion of Christian community. Both on a local and on a global scale.

New feelings shuffled in to replace the warmth I'd once felt while teamed with other Christians in ministry. I became almost embarrassed to be associated with institutional faith.

A couple of years prior, I never would have voiced such things out loud. Admitting that "sometimes I don't want to be part of the church" would have been like saying, "I think I'll become a Nazi" in some church circles.

On the contrary, if someone pointed out a chink in the church's shiny silver armor, I would rush forward and create some clever diversion. As the audience watched me dance and sing and tell jokes, their attention would be drawn away from the church's flaws long enough for the stagehands to rush in and apply some cover-up to Christianity's image.

But after experiencing my own religious meltdown, I could see our shortcomings everywhere, feeling brutally aware of the victims sometimes left in Christianity's wake. I began shifting more of my energy to understanding people outside the church, becoming acquainted with the stories of those who claimed no religious affiliation, and reading about renewing and repairing a sometimes broken or misrepresented religion.

I penned some fumbling essays about my frustrations with the church, eventually posting them on my website and sending them to a few friends. A few days later, I got a package from a twenty-six-year-old friend with whom I took a class while spending a semester in Chicago. Although we hadn't talked in several years, he took my essays along on a plane ride and ended up penning me a lengthy response.

On one page, he wrote: "My question is: Why should I stay in church? Why should I try to go through the disillusionment? What does the church offer that you can't get anywhere else?"

I began testing my observations against the experiences of other friends. The number and nature of responses I received in return caught me off guard. Not only were their replies usually immediate — sometimes shooting back to me in minutes and almost always within twenty-four hours — they were often incredibly intense. One person reported that she was so disheartened with her current church situation that she clocked out of work and took the morning off to read my essays. Another told me that he readily agreed with some of my perceptions, but he asked me not to let anyone at his church know that he had talked to me — lest someone see him as subversive and call for a pink slip. Several others sent email replies that spilled into pages and pages of feedback and personal stories, a few of which were lengthier than the essays themselves!

I even received emails from friends of the people I corresponded with, telling me, "I hope you don't mind that I wrote you, but my friend told me about your writing, and I am really interested in the topic." And almost without fail, each response included firsthand stories of his or her own frustrating experiences.

Rick, an online acquaintance, observed that my essays often seemed to associate disillusionment with my age: "I think much of what you say resonates with me, but frankly I feel a bit excluded in that I hardly qualify, at the age of forty-five, as one of the disillusioned twentysomethings. So I can't help but wonder if there's a way to say what you're saying but not limit your demographics to those twenty years younger.... Bottom line is, I encourage you to go forward but to also consider including the disillusioned who are a tad older. We're out there."

Rick's reaction to my essays wouldn't shock researchers. Observers have long been speculating that my generation can, in some ways, be considered an extension of the generation before them — both of whom are becoming less, not more, affiliated with the church.[3] In 1966 *Time* magazine ran the headline "Is God Dead?" As if an echo of the earlier story, *Newsweek* offered an article titled "The End of Christian America" in 2009.

In January 2012 the Barna Group reported that only 26 percent of Americans who had been to a church before said that their lives had been changed or affected "greatly" by attending church. Another one-fourth (25 percent) described it as "somewhat" influential. The largest number, nearly half, said their lives had not changed at all as a result of churchgoing (46 percent).[4]

And of course, church attendees are not the only ones disillusioned. Pastors and bishops are sometimes just as sick or sicker about religious dysfunction. One Duke Divinity School report titled "Experiences of Protestant Ministers Who Left Local Church Ministry" studied the most common motivations pastors cited for departing full-time ministry. Three of the top six reasons were rooted in internal church conflict: conflict or lack of support within the denomination, conflicts with church members, and doctrinal conflicts.[5]

This leads me back to the beginning: *You are not alone.* Though you may feel that way, there are many, many, *many* others fumbling through this same religious mire right this minute.

When we acknowledge or voice our frustrations with church or faith, we can be left feeling isolated. We may marvel at how everyone else who fills those sanctuary chairs each Sunday is able to hack it. How do they swallow the routine flaws that bother us so much? How do they keep forging ahead without pausing to blink in acknowledgment of what troubles us, what we lose sleep over? How do they manage such impeccable religious polish?

Their cheerful participation can be confounding.

Some of us have probably been abandoned or even ousted by Christian community, quite literally. Perhaps as you voiced your disagreements with the way faith has manifested itself in your setting, in our culture, or in history, your fellow believers not only have heaped criticism on your door but have privately or publicly cut ties with you.

Maybe you have been forced to deal with the contradictory and painful reality that former friends and teammates in ministry can walk away, claiming the name of Christ as they disappear into the distance.

You are not alone in these realities either.

Disillusionment belongs to all of us at one time or another. It is not a local problem, a regional problem, or a strictly generational problem. It is not an "us versus them" problem. Likely, at one point in time, we are all "us," becoming frustrated with the deficits of our religious experience at times. And likely — in other moments — we each have been "them," having positive, life-giving church experiences at times as well.

Everyone who is vested in the church, everyone who is serious about devoting his or her energies to advancing a local faith community, will at some point, to some extent, experience disillusionment. It is not an *if*; it is a *when*.

In the times we feel alone, it turns out, we are together even in that aloneness.

DISCUSSION QUESTIONS

1. Why do you think church attendees sometimes feel alone in their faith-related struggles? Is there a stigma to admitting you're struggling with ideas about God or faith? Explain your answer.

2. Could you relate to the author's story in having exceptionally good experiences within a church and perhaps holding that church community on too high of a pedestal? Have you seen or experienced that? Why do you think this happens?

3. Do you think it would be helpful to some who struggle to

have an understanding "grandmother" (or grandfather) type like the author described who could listen to them without sounding shocked or offering judgment? Has anyone been that kind of compassionate and patient supporter for you?

4. Do you agree with the author's suggestion that if you are deeply engaged in church for years, it is inevitable that you will experience some level of disappointment or frustration? Why or why not?

KEY IDEAS

◆ You are not alone. Research confirms many people of faith, including even church staff, become disillusioned over time.

◆ There is no singular antidote to church frustrations. Each person's faith story and related struggles are unique to that person.

Chapter 2

Don't Want to Be the Church Anymore

I have encountered many well-meaning, good-intentioned, brilliant, and sincere people whose lives are directed by faith. But despite that, and despite all my years in the Christian community, sometimes the word *church* just didn't feel right or good on my lips.

I wanted to whisper the word sometimes. Not because I'm ashamed but because, well, I know better than to be ashamed. Don't think I'm not aware of that verse.* (I can recite it in my best robotic KJV Scripture-memorizing voice, if you want.)

I wanted to whisper the word *church* because I knew that as soon as it left my mouth, someone in the room would flinch, inevitably thinking of extravagant steeples and crosses, angry people picketing in a parking lot, and road signs sporting interchangeable cheesy sayings. It's like playing one of those psychological games

---

* Romans 1:16.

where I say the word and everyone else says the first thing that comes to their minds. Only when I say "church," they tell me their reactions with their eyes, with their body language, and yes, sometimes with their mouths. And let's just say, positive reactions are sometimes hard to come by.

I wanted to whisper the word *church* because sometimes the person in the room who was flinching was me. Because despite all the amazing, mind-blowing images that come with any idea spoken into the world by Christ himself, the term *church* has developed some negative connotations even for me. So sometimes I resorted to saying it softly, or kind of half mumbling, half coughing it out into conversation without pausing to let someone point out that they can't understand my slurring.

Sometimes I just skip mentioning the C word altogether. Not to sell my faith short, but to get around all the assumptions attached to the label. Unfortunately, in our era it is not easy to describe your brand of Christian faith without affiliating yourself with a larger community.

Simply saying that I'm a Christian would be an immediate giveaway, of course. Christians go to church. Churches are full of Christians. Everyone sees the connection.

I can't really go around telling people I am "a person of the Way," because that brings to mind cults and stories of churches gone bad, like the cults of David Koresh and Jim Jones. Enough people already think the local Christian churches are cults.

I can't say I'm "an evangelical," because that, in many people's minds, is even worse than being a churchgoing Christian. To some, evangelicals are those people who preach a rotating list of twelve sermons all written to describe the eternal torment of hell. They are the people who play eerie music as the pastor asks people to raise their hands or "come forward." Or if they are on TV, maybe they ask you to touch the TV screen, where the static electric charge doubles as the spark of the Holy Spirit.

I can't say I'm "a conservative," because for some this beckons images of men with three-piece suits and neatly parted, unnaturally shiny hair who build coalitions to defeat the Democrats, the Smurfs, and billions of other alleged tools of Satan.

I can't say I'm "a progressive," because for some that lumps me in with some of the church's most prominent attackers, projecting me as a socialist vigilante who champions a list of pet causes and dismisses some or all of the Bible.

I can't say I'm "religious," because we've all been taught the folly of that. Now everyone say it together: "This is not a religion, it's a relationship." Although there are people like Lillian Daniel who are wise enough to poke holes in that trite little saying.[6]

I can't say I'm "spiritual," because people translate that as a simple "two thumbs up" for the latest movie with spiritual undertones. Or they figure I subscribe to an online horoscope and watch TV shows about channeling my dead pets. Spirituality is very in that way. My restaurant server, dry cleaner, dentist, and grocery store cashier all have religious wristbands and copies of the latest spiritual bestseller they picked up at the airport to prove it.

I wish I could land on a self-description that's new and fresh, something not so stained in people's minds. The only problem is, of course, that eventually too many followers of Christ (myself included) will show their humanness and our *new* words will be blacklisted from the usable list too.

Perhaps I should make it clear that *Christian* was never supposed to be a synonym for "perfect," or "never hypocritical." That is *Christ*. The two words come from the same root, and obviously there's an inescapable relationship between them. But mistaking even the best Christian for Christ is like seeing your first Model T and walking away thinking you've met Henry Ford.

DISCUSSION QUESTIONS

1. Do you relate to the author's discomfort with how Christians are stereotyped in culture? Why or why not?

2. Are you likely to volunteer information about your faith in Christ or leadership/membership in a church, or do you tend to wait to let that information come out? Why?

3. Which of the labels the author mentioned (such as "evangelical" or "progressive") or which labels she didn't mention are most problematic for you?

4. What kind of words do you use to describe your identity as a follower of Christ? What kind of language do you use when talking about being a person of faith or belonging to a church?

5. People tend to be surprised when church leaders or faith systems hurt others or fail, even though — as the author mentioned — Christians are always going to fall short of Jesus' example. Why do you think our culture has such high expectations of the church?

6. Do you think it is possible for a church to exist that does not in some way, at some level, disappoint others by failures or shortcomings? Why or why not?

KEY IDEAS

- ◆ One common difficulty of claiming your faith in the broader culture is that others may lump you in with the negative stereotypes of Christianity they have experienced.

- ◆ It is often helpful to separate Christians' behavior from the behavior of Christ. Although Christians seek to model the way of Jesus, if we expect them to be perfect, we will be disappointed every time.

Chapter 3

Know What
Disillusions You

F irst of all, I'm not sure you're even old enough to know what disillusionment is." This comment came during a Q&A following my presentation at a denominational con- ference. The format asked attendees to raise a hand or gesture to the microphone tech when they had a question. Then the sound crew member, discreetly dressed in black, was supposed to stealth- ily sneak the mic over to the attendee so the entire audience could hear his or her question.

Orrrrrr ... if you were this elderly southern pastor, one whose smile could be sugary-sweet while simultaneously having the body frame, light-colored polyester suit, and unchecked brazenness of Boss Hogg from *The Dukes of Hazzard*, you could just overpower all other commenters by barking your remarks loud enough for everyone to hear.

(Which, by the way, if you're the speaker who just delivered a presentation, is a surefire sign your Q&A is about to go really well.)

"Just how old were you when you wrote this thing?" He gestured at the cover of my first book, which was illuminated on the final slide displayed on the overhead screen.

(Second, you know, as a speaker, that your credibility is in trouble when the first questioner demands to know your age.)

I followed his gesture to the screen, suddenly wishing my photo that was used with the book looked less like a high school glamour shot.

There was no choice, of course, but to tell him the truth. "I was twenty-three when I wrote the book," I revealed in the most timelessly wise and mature voice I could muster. "But," I quickly added, "that was three years ago. I'm twenty-six now."

(I immediately felt like a child asserting she was three feet six and *a quarter* inches tall.)

I think what followed was some sort of holy grunt and sneer. Whatever the sound, it was immediately clear to me that Pastor Boss Hogg was the spiritual sheriff in these parts and I was not going to get any credit for having aged three whole years.

I had just delivered a presentation, one I'd grown pretty used to giving, on the topic of my first book, disillusionment among young people. It was a combination of illustrations, statistics, and ideas that I thought gave a comprehensive overview of the religious attitudes of my generation.

"Now, I'm going to tell you the one thing you didn't say."

(Third, it is a sign of great respect when your audience member shares that he is about to announce your flaws.)

"You didn't say just what it is all you young people are disillusioned about! Is it a local church? Do you people just buck all convention? Are you rejecting the Bible? What is it?"

"Frustrations are different for every person." I fumbled, half answering, half stalling. "What disillusions you may be different than what disillusions me. Maybe some people get disappointed because people groups get overlooked," I theorized. "Maybe they worry the church is caring for the Hebrew widows while the Greek widows are being neglected. Or maybe, if you go back to New Testament times, some people get mad because the senior missionary refuses to travel with the young recruit who left early on a previous trip."

(Tip: When addressing Boss Hogg pastors, it is always good to demonstrate you have heard of this Bible they speak of.)

"Or maybe some people get frustrated because those arrogant, think-they-know-everything young people like me have authority issues. Maybe we're too entitled, we lack perseverance or loyalty, we don't know the meaning of the word *duty*...." I paused to look at Pastor Boss Hogg with the feigned charm of a midwestern girl temporarily turned southern belle. "Am I getting close?"

He laughed then, which made me pretty sure I could've won him over if I had a few more minutes with him over straight black coffee and a couple of helpings of homemade cherry pie.

"Maybe young people like me make wise people like you, who've invested your whole lives in the church, sick to your stomach about where the faith is headed."

I shot him a raised eyebrow. *We're both kind of angry, aren't we?*

"The only way to know what someone is disillusioned about is to ask."

"Well, they ain't even around to ask!" he said sharply.

Now had I been a mere twenty-five and three-quarter years of age, this is probably where I would've tastelessly muttered something like, "Gee, I wonder why." But being all of twenty-six wise years of age, I had already decided that Boss Hogg was a good guy in defensive clothing. That he was maybe not so different than me, though he chose different words and even a different "style" to express it.

I was sad and cynical. He was perhaps mad and judgmental.

But he had showed, that day, the same thing I had shown in coming there.

Interest.

Which meant, especially combined with the fact that he bothered coming to my session, that he *cared*.

He, like me, cared that people were walking away from the church by the thousands.

I had lots of glaring immaturities, but I knew I needed the Pastor Boss Hoggs of the church. And I knew, just as surely, that I brought something to them too.

"You know," I said, "I think you're right."

(This he liked.)

"I think I missed a really obvious piece of this presentation. A question that is critical for people who feel disillusioned with church. *And* a question equally important for people like you, who try to serve them."

I turned to the rest of the audience, also known as eyewitnesses in the event Pastor Boss Hogg happened to be brandishing a southern-fried shotgun. "How do we know how to respond to disillusionment if we don't know what caused it in the first place?" I asked them.

"How ya gonna fix something if you don't know what's broke?" Pastor Boss Hogg turned toward the audience too as he chimed in, as if we were giving the presentation together.

"Amen," I said.

After that, no one else asked a single question. I'm pretty sure it was because they recognized that Pastor Boss Hogg was the law in the room.

And that, at least for that moment, didn't turn out to be such a bad thing.

In retrospect, I wonder if I left out a review of what sorts of things disillusion people because if someone asked me, I wouldn't have known the answer for myself … let alone my generation. Beginning on the plane ride home from my speaking engagement, though, I settled in to search for my own answers to this question.

In reviewing my own disappointing experiences, I felt like the feature patient in an episode of *House*, the TV series about a quirky but gifted doctor whose team of medical investigators try to solve the most bizarre illnesses that arise at the fictional Princeton – Plainsboro Teaching Hospital.

In this medical drama, the medical team first lists all the patient's symptoms on a whiteboard. *Swelling, achy joints, fever, infection.* Then they spend the whole episode trying to figure out if the symptoms are connected. Are they all results of the same illness? Or, when they learn the patient just went on a twelve-mile hike into the Grand Canyon the day before, should they attribute the swelling and achy joints to fatigue and just focus on the fever and infection?

Of course the patients themselves aren't always objective about their own conditions. They sometimes misremember their recent routines, accidentally leave out something important, or purposefully lie to cover up their own misbehaviors.

Disillusionment is that same kind of complicated. A mess of emotions is involved. There are multiple kinds of frustration caused by multiple kinds of sources. And as with the medical patients, pain can skew our ability to objectively reflect on our own condition.

Nevertheless, in writing and talking about this topic for more than ten years now, I feel it is safe to say most disillusionment can be categorized using at least one of the following descriptors.

1. *We're disillusioned with one person or a small group of people, localized to where we live or where we have interacted.* When it's just one person who lets us down, people may not take our disappointment seriously. Our experience may seem unimportant to an outsider, like just one tiny dot on the landscape of life or spirituality. But often this one person or small group of people holds disproportionate weight in our lives because we had immense respect for them. Perhaps they were the ones who first embodied Christ to us or who first engaged us in the mission of the church. Perhaps we see them as mentors, as spiritual mothers and fathers.

2. *We're disillusioned by an action.* This is sort of like the first case, in that we may actually be disillusioned by just one single action in the chain of thousands of life events, but even though we may not respect or assign importance to the people, the act itself derails us. Whether it is an unfortunate judgment made by a religious leader we only knew slightly or someone whom we have always detested for years of spiritual manipulation or abuse, the act or acts themselves — the fact a spiritual leader could molest a child or defraud a congregation or abandon his family — seem to say all we need to know about the church.

3. *We're disillusioned by a local congregation.* Often this is actually number one in disguise. Because one person or small group hurt us so badly, we write off the larger body of people even though — if we are really honest — most of them had nothing to do with our frustrations. But sometimes it is some practice of the majority, the way the church as a whole spends money, the way it treats women, the way it shames certain members or visitors, that

we find exclusionary or harmful. Or perhaps it is a case of collective neglect. Out of an entire congregation, no one noticed when we stopped attending for four weeks, or no one even came to the hospital when we had that surgery.

4. *We're disillusioned by an entire denomination or larger grouping.* Perhaps we have become angry toward or divided from an entire denomination or an entire style of church. Perhaps we're angry at every Lutheran, all the Baptists, or the whole lot of seeker churches or emergent gatherings. Maybe we're up in arms about the Pentecostals, the conservatives, or the liberals. Again, we often assign things to this category that more rightly belong in category 3, because we've allowed our experience with one charismatic church or one Reformed church to give us a bad taste for all.

But there are some of us who truly are disillusioned with entire denominations or camps. Perhaps we've been very involved in the more macro scene; we've been the one going to all those state conventions, denominational conferences, and official assemblies. Maybe we've rubbed up against dozens or hundreds of Christians from across the globe who identify with the same group and we have gained a distaste for the way in which they express their faith.

5. *We're disillusioned by all traditional churches.* We've decided, based on our experience with one church or with many congregations of different kinds in different places that these modern-day expressions of church just don't cut it. We reject the routine of meeting in buildings; of holding once-a-week, hour-long services; of paying pastors; or of adhering to some other methodology. We think the modern, Western model or some other model is a poor or ineffective reflection of Christian community.

6. *We're disillusioned by all expressions of organized faith.* This includes those who do not attend church but still consider

themselves people of the Christian faith. While we don't claim membership anywhere, perhaps we run soup kitchens, lead protests on Capitol Hill, feel God out in nature, and find his ideas in movies and songs from pop culture. We reject all organized expressions of faith, and we dislike institutions of any kind. We will not go to small groups or house churches. We will not become card-carrying members of any movement, no matter what side of postmodernity it is on. We refuse to believe that something as sacred as spirituality can be mechanized. Period.

7. *We're disillusioned with Christianity as a religion.* We still believe in the message of the Bible, but we don't think it was ever intended to birth what it did — this enormous group of power holders with the endless lists of doctrines, factions, and denominations. We like to say we're following in the way of Jesus; we are schema people who love God and love people. Our mantra is "Take your religion and shove it. We want to sit at the feet of our Teacher."

8. *We're disillusioned by doctrines any number of sources have attached to the Christian faith.* There's something on the books, something on the "We Believe" page, something about the way we're too Calvinistic or too Armenian, something about how sin is defined or how right behavior is assessed, something about how God is portrayed. Something. Or maybe we think the beliefs embraced as doctrine don't really capture what the Bible says. We just can't buy it. It seems old, antiquated, and irrelevant, and/or it seemingly contradicts our own reading of the Scripture, our reason, conscience, or experience.

9. *We're disillusioned with God himself.* This is not to say we don't believe in God. We may, or in the most extreme cases, we may not. But in any sense, we're angry with him for any number of things — usually for showing so much restraint, rather than inter-

vening, when people suffer or are abused. We're disappointed God doesn't seem to give us adequate support, that he seems to give us too many burdens to bear, that he seems to require us to meet too many demands, that he abandoned us as children to some horrible reality, or that he lets pompous powermongers carry his banner in the parades of life.

10. *We're disillusioned with life in general.* Perhaps we're just angry, angry that life didn't turn out the way we wanted. Upset that existence on earth plays out the way it does. That everyone's body degenerates, that everyone dies, that good people suffer sometimes while evil people flourish. Maybe we have become demotivated, depressed, and run-down, without hope about anything or anyone in general. And when we carry so much bitterness, we reject all institutions or ideas that claim to bear hope, including the church.

You have likely picked up from my commentary, or from your own experience, that these ten things that disappoint us are often intertwined with each other. While there may be a scale of disillusionment that starts in one category, it often soon spreads to others. And everyone's journey, their escalations or de-escalations, which categories they dip into or don't dip into, are different too.

One thing is certain though: *no one can understand our disillusionment for us.* We must examine our emotions and experiences for ourselves.

DISCUSSION QUESTIONS

1. Have you ever been dismissed by a church leader or person of faith who looked down on you for your frustrations? Or have you seen this attitude expressed toward other people who have expressed disillusionment?

2. Why do you think church people sometimes react angrily to those who are struggling with church?

3. What do you think would help church leaders like Pastor Boss Hogg get to know and understand the disillusioned more?

4. Do you know what disillusions you? Of the ten things the author mentions can be a source of frustration for people, which ones do you relate to? Are there others you can think of that are not listed?

5. Has there ever been a time when you were so angry or overcome with negative emotions that you could not even objectively identify what was wrong? What kind of advice would you give to someone who is so consumed with bitterness or disappointment that they can't even think straight?

KEY IDEAS

◆ Disillusionment is not new to our time. People have experienced it stretching back through generations of church history, even likely to biblical times.

◆ Oftentimes those who are disillusioned outside the church and those inside the church who are frustrated with disillusioned people share some of the same emotions, such as anger or disappointment, that the church experience did not turn out the way they'd hoped.

◆ Sometimes when people appear to be angry or frustrated, it is a good sign because it indicates that they care about the problem at hand and feel it deep in their emotions.

◆ Every person's reasons for disillusionment are slightly different based on his or her specific experiences.

◆ People may be disillusioned with one thing, or sometimes many reasons pile up to contribute to their frustrations. There may not be one simple cause for their disillusionment, just as there may not be one easy answer.

◆ Sometimes people's negative emotions can impair their ability to be objective and reasonably assess their own experiences. It is possible, then, that they do not even know what disillusions them or that they at least can't easily put it into words.

Chapter 4

Let It Go

I wasn't convinced the church leaders among you would still be reading at this point. Not that I think you're short on stamina, but I worried that if I mentioned disillusionment one too many times, this book might "accidentally" get incinerated during a reckless night of campfires, s'mores, and "Kumbayah."

Don't worry though. I couldn't vent about my own frustrations forever, even if I wanted to. Frankly, I couldn't keep up the stamina to maintain such cynicism.

In the beginning, I needed to grieve my disappointments with the church. I needed to name what went wrong, to learn from it and seek healing. In that early stage, being cynical even felt misleadingly good. I was relieved to finally say what was troubling me. I felt empowered when I advocated for more wholesome, less harmful ways of functioning as a church than what I'd sometimes experienced. It felt good — in the worst of prideful ways — to rehearse why I thought I was right and some other people were wrong. Rolling my eyes while taking jabs at flawed church structures and people of faith who rubbed me the wrong way was more than a little bit satisfying.

But somewhere along the way, that false sense of good started unraveling. As the tension inside me grew, there came a scary tipping point when I began spending more of my life being disgruntled than living in hope. In fact, I would say my commitment to disillusionment bordered, at times, on idolatry. When I let my dissatisfaction with church direct how I responded to people or events, I would in effect turn the day over to disillusionment. And every time I allowed myself to be influenced by these same disappointments, I gave disillusionment another day. Before long, I'd unintentionally pledged weeks, months, maybe even years to discontentment. I began to give my life not to Jesus but to my frustration with his people.

This kind of unexpected idolatry — the obsession with living in despair over what is wrong with institutionalized church — crept up on me (like most shifty little idols do). No one ever asked me to repeat a prayer and ask disillusionment into my life. No one ever asked me to read a membership manual explaining my ongoing commitment to disillusionment. Just the same, criticism almost became what I was worshiping. And it felt anything but good. The fact that I couldn't breathe or blink or just "be" without feeling jaded made life seem like a scary Ferris wheel ride. I felt trapped in a car stuck halfway up with no chance to move forward or to get out and see the world from a different perspective.

I realized, suddenly, that my complaints against the church weren't righting the world any faster than my allegiance to it. All my venting and railing didn't erase the church's imperfections or resolve the hypocrisy of any group of believers (including my own). Being jaded and skeptical no longer felt good. It was no longer giving me a high.

Somewhere around the time when I reached this point, I found myself in an obscure conversation with a surgeon friend who told me, "I never meet patients who've been doing crack or meth for thirty years. I see that kind of long-term use with marijuana but not with the harder drugs. If people used that stuff over a prolonged period of time, they'd be dead, hospitalized, or locked up. The body just isn't capable of staying healthy and functional if it is exposed to certain toxic substances for prolonged periods of time."

His words had immediate implications for my situation. Disillusionment, I realized, had become one of those toxic substances. My spirit was just not capable of staying healthy and functional when exposed to this toxicity for prolonged periods of time.

It was time to let it go.

Although typing those three little words — "let it go" — into a book years later is easy, at the time, in the middle of my frustrations, it felt insanely hard to release the negative emotions around my experience. Some of you understand what I mean by that. You're still writhing in pain so much that you can't read the suggestion that there may come a time to "let it go" without balking at it.

For me to even suggest that "letting it go" is part of the healing process may even seem insensitive — as if I, someone who has said I can deeply relate to your angst, am now betraying you by seemingly implying that you are doing something wrong or that you, the victim in some cases, must be the one to change in some way.

I acknowledge that. Similar points of resistance once ran through my mind, and I've heard similar worries from disillusioned audiences for years. Things like this:

> If I let it go, that is inauthentic. That is like pretending [insert harmful act that happened in church] didn't happen or, worse yet, pretending it was okay.

If I let it go, the offender or the church leadership or the congregation may never realize what happened; they may never be aware of the wrong that has taken place.

If I let it go, the situation will not be righted. The offending party will not be confronted or corrected, the structure of the church will not be repaired, the offender will keep offending free and clear.

If I let it go, I will never get personal resolution. The relationships that have been damaged will never be repaired, reconciliation will never happen, apologies will never be given, and I will never feel better.

If I let it go, then I am giving up. I am putting up a white flag and letting injustice prevail. I am not fighting for the side of right, and therefore I'm not contributing to helping the church heal or regain strength for the future.

Believe me, I get it. As someone whose heart now feels free and light again, and as someone who now wishes I would have left my jaded state of being behind *far earlier* than I did, I have to tell you: it's worth pushing past the resistance.

There are many solid reasons for letting go of the emotions around your frustrations, but for now let's just start with the easiest reason to swallow: you want to feel well again.

You do, right?

You really do want to and maybe even *need* to feel well again. And all the negative emotion isn't helping that happen. In the moments we spend revisiting our injuries, analyzing and critiquing others' behavior, and reciting our grievances to our friends, we are not erasing the negativity in our past. We are instead sacrificing valuable time and energy to negativity.

Dwelling on the hardship tied to our church experience and letting the negative feelings about it consume us does not punish the offending person or system. They likely go on about their days unfazed by the struggle we're enduring. The overanalyzing and reviewing punishes us alone, locking us into a self-made and self-maintained prison, a state of being miserable and frustrated as a perpetual religious victim.

And don't worry. Laying down these bitter emotions is not the same thing as giving up your desire to see wrongs remedied. It's just giving up your desire to let unremedied wrongs prolong the negative impact they have had on your life.

While you cannot force other people involved in your church history to lay down their negative emotions that may be blocking good from prevailing, you can do your part to release your own emotional baggage. You can cut yourself free from the bitterness and anger that entangle you so that if opportunity presents itself, your clear mind and balanced emotional state will enable you to better help bring about reconciliation or justice.

Maybe you can even try to see "letting it go" as a small act of faith. An act of surrender. An opportunity to say to yourself and anyone who is watching, "I recognize that I am not in control of this situation, that I cannot reverse what has happened or mandate other parties to act with goodwill. Nor can I force change or repentance or growth to occur at the pace of my choosing. God has not placed me in a position of high enough authority that I can correct this situation by myself, but that also means my burden can be lighter, for I am only responsible for the part I am capable of changing. I will trust that this act of obedience — of laying down my right to be consumed by negative emotions and recommitting the energy I'm freeing up to God — will result in good at least for me and maybe for others."

Even though this one act of letting go will not right the entire situation, you may be surprised at how transforming the decision to "let go" can be. One of the best ways to stave off cynicism and skepticism, it turns out, is with faith.

I have been asked many times at conferences or churches what I wish people had said to me in the throes of my disillusionment. And my answer, though I would probably be hesitant to speak it so bluntly to someone else, is always the same: "I think at first I needed space and permission to bring my frustrations to expression. But very quickly after that, I became so bitter, I was almost my own worst enemy. So I don't know if I would have listened. But if I could go back and talk to my younger self, I could sum up what I personally needed to hear in three sentences: *Buck up and grow up, Sarah. You cannot move forward until you let go of what is behind you. It will be hard, but do it anyway.*"

DISCUSSION QUESTIONS

1. Can you relate to the author's description of idolatry? In what ways might our frustrations take time away from our worship of God or the lifestyle Jesus calls us to?

2. What was your reaction when the author suggested she had to "let it go"? Did it seem relieving to consider the thought of finally setting down any negative emotions you're carrying? Or did it seem pressuring, like someone is insisting you set aside something that troubles you before you are ready?

3. Have you ever experienced what the author described as living in a "self-made and self-maintained prison," making yourself a perpetual victim by continually forcing yourself to revisit and relive bad experiences?

4. What is the biggest obstacle that stands between you and being able to let go?

5. Most of us want to see the wrong or harmful experiences we've witnessed remedied in some way. What part of your negative experiences is your responsibility to remedy? What parts are outside of your control and must be "let go" to God or other parties?

6. What do you think of Sarah's final words to her younger self: "Buck up and grow up, Sarah. You cannot move forward until you let go of what is behind you. It will be hard, but do it anyway." Have there been times when it would have been helpful for someone to say these words to you? Why or why not?

KEY IDEAS

◆ The amount of time we give to rehearsing our disillusionment can, after a time, shift our life away from being devoted to Jesus to instead being devoted to expressing our anger or unhappiness.

◆ While it is difficult to let go of negative emotions, it may be helpful to do it not because we feel pressured by others but because it is in our own best interest.

◆ A person's spirit is not capable of staying healthy and functional when exposed to toxic substances for prolonged periods of time.

◆ Laying down these bitter emotions is not the same thing as giving up your desire to see wrongs remedied. It's just giving up your desire to let unremedied wrongs prolong the negative impact they have had on your life.

- Letting go may be hard, and we may not be eager to do it, but those who have been through such experiences have found it is important to press through the difficulty and do it anyways.

- People often find that after releasing negative emotions, they become better balanced and more prepared to help work out a solution later.

Chapter 5

The Road beyond the Broken Church

As we intentionally stop revisiting our negative emotions, we may slowly discover that disillusionment has not only altered our mood but also impacted how we look at ourselves and how we perceive where and with whom we belong.

During some of my worst moments, for example, I found that I began to detach from the people in the church's pulpits and seats. I'd seen enough bad unfold at the hand of these organized faith systems that I wanted no part of them.

I began to disidentify with many in traditional church contexts. *I am not this institutional church type, this organized religion type; I am not a drone in an institutional faith system that sometimes abuses its power or damages people in hypocritical ways. I am some other sort of faith-being altogether.*

With little intention, I quickly defaulted into membership with another more loosely affiliated group, a group of ex-churched or marginally churched people who seemed to exist in reaction to the first. I began to find common ground with this vast and growing group of religiously disaffected people — some local, some living elsewhere in the country — who identified as religiously disillusioned.

They too felt some of the same outrage I did. They too were angry at exclusion, frustrated by hypocrisy, up in arms about abuses of power. They too had borne burdens, championed the disadvantaged, endured pain. And they too thought it was funny to poke fun at the sometimes cheesy, hyper-structured, or image-managed church culture. These disaffected people were easy companions in a time when I felt mostly alone.

And somewhere along the way, while immersed among my fellow cynics and skeptics, I concluded this — this jaded, anti-institutional being — was the new me. This was my identity. I was one of "the disillusioned."

The only problem was, I was dead wrong. While I had experienced disappointment with the church and was saddened by the hardship and discouragement it brought me, I eventually came to see it was not healthy or life giving to label myself as "disillusioned." To identify myself as disillusioned, for example, made it seem as though my current state was unchangeable and I was powerless to find different or better ground. Even worse, choosing a hopeless identifier like "disillusioned" was a bit contradictory for someone like me who claimed to be a person of "faith." I thought, *How can someone like me who claims to believe in a loving Creator and chooses to look at this world through a filter of faith adopt* cynical *or* disillusioned *as her primary personal descriptor?*

And even if it had made sense, why would I want to? Why choose to self-identify with such a discouraging state? To shore up my life in sadness — in unbelonging and isolation? In anti-this and anti-that? Why not identify with the many positives — my good, strong personality traits; my penchant for learning; my hunger to know the reality of this God I was trekking after? Perhaps together, if I held on to them, these good things might disarm or reduce the power of the negative emotions I was experiencing. I had experienced disillusionment, but it was not who I was.

It may sound like a technicality, but in my case, the language surrounding my emotions was tied to the way I understood myself and others. Moving from "I am disillusioned" to "I am experiencing disillusionment" was the first of many shifts necessary for me to move forward sanely.

My perception of myself had such significant ramifications for my healing because it impacted how I believed I fit (or did not fit) in relationship with others who claimed the name of Christ. Identifying myself as anti-this-church or anti-this-system reinforced my otherness; it exacerbated my apartness from the larger community of Jesus followers in which I had been raised. Changing the way I thought of myself helped ease my sometimes perhaps exaggerated perceptions of isolation and divisiveness.

By revoking my own license to claim some sort of "other status," I curbed my tendency to project tension onto all religious communities and organized expressions of faith. It took the wind out of the self-absorbed "us versus them" battle I was always prepping for. *People in the church are so this way. We have to get them to see the error of their ways.* It gave me permission to see good in people of faith, to find allies — even in churches and institutions — again.

Most plainly, understanding that being disillusioned was just a stage and not an identity, made me a more likable person to be around. I wasn't always positioning myself against something or reacting to something. I was on the lookout for hope. I was counting down the days to when I felt less tension and could breathe easier and feel more common ground with traditional faith communities again.

And finally, dropping my status as "disillusioned" freed me to stop looking at disillusionment as an unchangeable identity and instead try to find the opportunity inside of this temporary stage. What I learned, to my amazement, was that even though our culture tends to view the word *disillusionment* as a negatively charged word, it is actually quite the opposite. The prefix *dis* in Latin means "away from" or "apart." And *illusion* means "a false impression of reality." To be disillusioned, then, is *to move away from a false impression of reality*. So disillusionment isn't something to be avoided at all costs. It is in fact desirable, *even necessary*. After all, who — if given a choice — would want to live their entire lives clinging to false impressions of reality?

To the contrary, it's possible our lives would be best served and our faith most strengthened if we saw disillusionment as a vehicle that took us beyond the broken church to something better. How much healthier might our expressions of faith be, for instance, if we could unwrap ourselves from fraudulent ideas like "My pastor is perfect," "Being a Christian means things will always go my way," or "Being in Christian community means Christian values will always be applied"? Moving away from these mistaken and lesser ideas might, in the end, be the very thing that allows us to adopt realistic expectations that can help our faith to survive for years to come.

How relieved pastors and denominational leaders might be if they looked at disillusionment not as a crisis but as an opportunity for us to dig deeper, examine our beliefs, press into God, and search out the best he has for us! And how much stronger and healthier might expressions of church be if we allowed disillusionment to alert us to actions that don't align with God's intentions or behaviors, to help expose components that aren't even congruent with our own stated objectives.

Disillusionment actually becomes a redeeming process if we let it serve in this sort of prompting role in our lives. It can fast-forward the growth of our convictions, giving us the extra push and courage to stand up and say, "This is not how church should be. This is not what God wants people to experience in his community." It can inspire us to get off our religiously bogged-down booties and actually do something to help better represent God's purposes to our world.

In my life, in some strange way, God has used disillusionment not to lay me to rest in brokenness, but to move me beyond it, to employ disillusionment for his ends. I now believe that in his grand and free and more nuanced economy, he deliberately let me endure the ups and downs of the pendulum swings, allowed me to wade in the ebb and flow of the surging waves, until I exhausted myself in the struggle to achieve balance. This tension between who I am and who I am striving to become has kept me active and engaged and hungry to learn and invest in the faith.

As Pastor Andy Stanley says, "Anyone who is emotionally involved — frustrated, brokenhearted, maybe even angry — about the way things are in the light of the way they believe things could be, is a candidate for vision. Visions form in the hearts of those who are dissatisfied with the status quo."[7] Disillusionment thus became a prerequisite for maintaining my spiritual vitality. Tension and frustration breathed life into my quest to know our Creator rather than resigning me to walk mindlessly in the footsteps of those who had gone down the path that leads away from God and the church before me. If you are disillusioned or your congregation, ministry, or denomination has lost many to disillusionment, do not panic. Disillusionment may likely be part of people's growing pains, a needed rite of passage that propels their spiritual growth.

As biblical scholar N. T. Wright is fond of saying, "Each generation has to wrestle afresh with the question of Jesus, not least its biblical roots if it is to be truly the church at all."[8]

Disillusionment, for many, is the road to what lies beyond the broken church.

DISCUSSION QUESTIONS

1. Have you ever considered yourself to be one of "the disillusioned"? What do you think motivated you to identify with those who are cynical or disappointed with the church?
2. Can you understand why the author said she needed companions to relate to during a time when she felt alone? Why or why not?
3. Can you see why the author thinks it is important to distinguish the difference between "being disillusioned" and "experiencing disillusionment"? Which one feels more permanent?
4. Have you ever wanted to distance yourself from Christians who caused you disappointment? Did you ever find a way to feel some sort of belonging with them again? If you did, what kind of things helped you get to a place where you could feel commonality with them again?
5. Is it helpful to think about the definition of disillusionment being "to move away from false impressions of reality"? What false impressions of reality might you or others who are frustrated with the church need to move away from?

KEY IDEAS

- After a disillusioning experience, people may feel distanced from their church community. This newfound loneliness may prompt them to seek companionship with others who can relate to their struggles.

- Frustrated people may, even subconsciously, look for a new group of people to replace the old one and therefore begin to identify themselves as "antichurch" or "disillusioned."

- Referring to oneself as "disillusioned" or spending time with other people who are currently feeling little hope is not helpful. Doing so reinforces negativity in your life and possibly prevents people who are feeling good about church to balance your perspective with more optimism.

- Thinking of yourself as "disillusioned" may make this disappointed stage of your life feel like a permanent part of your identity rather than a temporary struggle that will pass in time.

- Disillusionment is often viewed as a crisis, but it can also be an opportunity to move away from false impressions of reality toward healthier, more realistic expectations for the church.

Chapter 6

Wise Counselor

I know. I know. Even when positioned as an "opportunity" rather than a crisis, overcoming disillusionment is just not that simple. It's not a twenty-four-hour flu bug that disappears after a day of rest and fluids.

It is more chronic than that.

Disillusionment is a serious illness of the soul. It tends to persist over a long, indefinite period of time and often involves multiple recurrences. And it can be virtually invisible to people who meet you, so much so that people in your local church might not even realize you're infected.

And we may not realize the epidemic we're up against.

I'm not sure we'd know if our sanctuaries were overflowing with people in the throes of disillusionment ... because many of us are phenomenal actors. Working without a script, we ad-lib our way through the Sunday morning church routine with Oscar-worthy performances.

We know how to work a sanctuary. How to walk down the

red — or sometimes tacky, multicolored Berber — carpet shaking hands, kissing babies, and giving people quick squeezes. We know how to flash a winning smile and how to project just the right tone of voice when we offer hellos and greet with "How are you?" We know to call people by their first names and to try to make personal comments that make them feel important.

We can be schmoozing machines.

But despite our professional Christianity, despite our wealth of brownie points within the volunteer pool in our local congregation, we are deep in the fight to release false impressions of reality, to own that we are hurting and that our church is full of polished but still fatally flawed and unhealthy people.

I don't know why our own dysfunction is so surprising. We expect slip-ups from other groups of people — lawyers, car salespeople, politicians, or celebrities, but when it comes to the church, we're complete suckers. Or at least I am.

I don't know why I think anyone with the ability to match their clothes, read the Bible, and teach without stuttering also must have a pure thought life and be impervious to temptation. I don't know why I think anyone with a great singing voice, a standard acoustic guitar, and a little rock and roll must have an amazing devotional life and a carefree marriage. I don't know why I think people who have mastered the art of passing out bulletins have risen above anger management classes, gossip, and parenting problems. And most of all, I don't know why I think that just because people come together and buy their own building in the name of Christ, they will always — without fail — act like true representatives of Christ.

Could I get any more unrealistic?

Sometimes I wonder how my experience with church would

change if I could just make a few mental adjustments. What would happen, for example, if I honestly admitted that I am likely to encounter one or more of the following church flaws?

At some point, church people *may ...*

- not always appreciate my giftedness, my skill sets, or even my service to the church.
- not always take the time to understand where I'm coming from.
- not always care about some of the things I value most.
- not always offer the kind of support I need when I need it.
- pressure me to live up to their expectations.
- turn my mistakes or grief into material for gossip.
- act in a way that seems "fake."
- get caught up with the wrong priorities.
- exercise power to exclude or dismiss.
- do things in their personal lives that make me admire them less.
- make bad decisions that end up hurting the church.
- seem to ignore, misread, or misapply certain portions of Scripture.
- not notice when I'm absent or sick or hurting.
- make me feel judged or abandoned.

Is it possible that just by changing some of my expectations, I could influence my own ability to contentedly engage Christian community? If I simply realized that every church or group of people — no matter how exciting or brilliant — is infested with all kinds of flaws, would I respond to their failures differently? Would I draw different conclusions?

Instead of seeing apparent failures as a contradiction of all the church stands for, instead of seeing them as reason to throw out institutionalized church as a whole, instead of seeing them as evidence that the ideals of God himself might somehow be tainted, what if I just thought, *Yes, I'm disappointed. This is further evidence of human ability to make unhealthy choices. But this is not surprising. And while we grieve it, we can choose to limit the time and energy we give to despair. We can seek to learn from our pain and failures, and to apply our learning to living more fully in the future.*

Along these lines, I've decided that maybe the church should introduce a type of "premarital counseling" for people considering commitment. Here's how I imagine it would work.

> *You walk into a room. There, sitting behind an official-looking desk, is an especially wise counselor wearing a very serious pair of glasses, pen and clipboard in hand.*

> *You feel a little uneasy.*

> *Wise Counselor introduces himself and then gets right into the session. "So, tell me why you think you want to commit to this congregation."*

> *You freeze. You know there are absolutely tons of things you love about this congregation, but you're worried you won't be able to convey the true breadth of your adoration in a couple of concise, convincing statements.*

> *"Well, I really appreciate the emphasis on the Word of God," you say, hoping that calling the Bible the "Word of God" will get you a few extra points.*

> *Wise Counselor doesn't say much. Just an "uh-huh" as he checks something on the paper in front of him.*

> *Apparently he wants you to say more.*

"And I really enjoy the people. The community, I mean fellowship, is so important to me." You chide yourself for almost forgetting to use the word fellowship.

Wise Counselor nods. You go on.

"Not to mention I love the worship. The song leader is very talented. She really knows how to invite the congregation into the presence of God."

You allow yourself a quick smile, feeling like you've touched on all the religious bases.

Wise Counselor raises a suspicious eyebrow in your direction. He sets aside the clipboard with the evaluation that you may have just failed and stares at you. He seems to be purposely trying to increase the amount of awkward tension in the room.

Just when you think Wise Counselor's eyes have bored a hole into your inner thought chamber and you are about to confess that as a toddler you colored on Jesus' face in your children's Bible storybook, he finally cuts the silence.

And then you wish he wouldn't have said anything at all.

Wise Counselor leans forward. "Now tell me some of your church's flaws."

"Um ..." You stall while analyzing all your possible responses. If you say you think your church has no flaws, you will certainly seem like you're caught up in blind love. But if you say it has too many, it might seem like your love is insincere.

"Well, sometimes the Sunday morning coffee runs out before everyone has a cup."

This seems like a safe place to start.

You can tell Wise Counselor is not impressed.

"And, um, I've noticed that on certain weeks there are some particularly obvious typos on the media screen."

He's tapping his fingers and gazing into space. Boring.

"Not to mention that sometimes there is a really loud microphone thud or a lot of feedback over the speakers. You hear this high-pitched squeal, and then you see the service producer calling back on the telephone to tell the sound guys to get their act together."

Now you're getting to the good stuff.

But Wise Counselor is tough to win over.

He stares at you a moment longer, as if summoning the right amount of emotion to deliver his next lines.

"But what if one day the sermons get boring? Let's say, perchance, they don't seem to relate to you."

You gulp.

"Let's say your fellow attendees don't seem to care about you at all! Let's say they just seem to be using you to get you to serve those horrible fifth graders whom no one wants to teach in next year's vacation Bible school?"

You try to hold still, but you know you are visibly squirming in your chair.

"Let's say one day the worship leader goes tone deaf. What would happen if she suddenly couldn't sing on key, or worse yet, if she started singing every single verse of every hymn in slow motion?"

You wonder if you're supposed to respond, but you pray the questions are rhetorical.

"What if the pastor fails you?

"What if the nursery leader runs off with the head usher?

"What if the church uses your tithe to buy thousands of burger flipper souvenirs for their upcoming message series 'Serving It Up God's Way'?

"What if it gets to the point that you can't invite your pastor and your worship leader, your board members, or your Sunday school teachers to the same Christmas party because of how much they distrust and dislike each other?"

Your mind is spinning in a million directions.

"Do you love your church enough to stick with them through all of that? Do you love them enough to love them even when the emotions run low and the feelings of excitement have worn off?"

Wise Counselor's voice is increasingly louder. The lights above his desk seem especially hot.

"Are you in this for better or for worse, for richer or for poorer, in sickness and in health?" As he spits out these last words, Wise Counselor's fist slams down on the desk, creating a small earthquake that disrupts all the papers.

Slowly, out of the corner of your eye, you begin looking for the nearest emergency exit.

Then, just as suddenly as it rose, Wise Counselor's voice softens.

"I'm not trying to scare you away or anything," he drawls in a mild-mannered tone.

You manage to nod even though you wish you could curl up in the fetal position.

Wise Counselor continues, "But you can't let anyone tell you that committing to a church is all fantasies and fairy-tale endings. You can't think that once you become a member things are going to magically fall into place, that every day is going to be one more day of happily ever after.

"Committing to a church isn't easy. It takes a lot of hard work. You're not perfect. Your church isn't perfect. A lot of imperfect things are going to happen along the way. Sure, you're going to have your exhilarating highs, but you're going to have some rock-bottom lows too.

"You're going to encounter some flaws in the church that you never knew about or suspected. You're going to see that the church doesn't really value all the things they claim to value. Someday you're going to start to feel like the church is a totally different organization than it was before you committed to membership. You're going to wake up one day and wonder what possessed you to join the place."

Wise Counselor smiles. "Once the honeymoon stage ends, then what do you do?"

You don't even try to answer this one.

Thankfully, Wise Counselor likes to hear himself talk.

"You might think about leaving the church. But if you do, just remember, every church has its own set of flaws. Sure, you might find another church that seems attractive, that seems to excel in the areas where your church falters, but beware! If you join another church, you won't find the perfect church; you'll just find a completely different set of flaws.

"Scared? Good!"

You're noticing Wise Counselor has a flair for the dramatic.

"But, thankfully, you know who to run to when you're scared. Ultimately, you see, your commitment is not to this one local church. In fact, your commitment is not even to the global ideal, the church at large. Your commitment is to God. And as long as you nurture your relationship with God and you draw closer to him, you will also find the ability to sustain your relationship with your local church."

And then, with one statement — "We're going to give you a couple of weeks to think this over" — Wise Counselor's spiel is over. He hands over a waiver to sign so your church can prove that someone has explained the potential risks involved in joining their congregation if you decide to do so.

DISCUSSION QUESTIONS

1. Do you agree with the author's suggestion that churches might not even know if some of their attendees are disillusioned due to the expectation that everyone interact according to social norms?

2. Have you or anyone you've known had unrealistic expectations of church at any point? What do you think are some of the most common mistaken expectations people might have of their faith communities?

3. How have you tried to adjust your expectations to be realistic and better equip you to deal with disappointment without sacrificing the importance of trying to foster the healthiest and most God-honoring Christian community you can?

4. Do you think the average person sees church as a lifetime commitment similar to marriage? Why or why not? And if not, how do they look at their commitment or relationship to the church in your opinion?

KEY IDEAS

◆ It is not always easy to detect disillusionment in churches, because people may feel pressured to act upbeat or at least "fine" in order to protect their reputation as Christian leaders.

◆ Christians sometimes set themselves up for disappointment because they are not prepared for the moments when churches, which are made up of flawed human beings, let them down.

◆ If we adjust our expectations to allow for normal human error and fallibility, we will still be disappointed by failure and hardship but will likely be better positioned to integrate tough moments into our overall faith journey and carry on.

◆ It can be helpful to see our relationship to the church as being like a lifelong relationship to a spouse or even a parent, child, or sibling; to view it as a relationship that will include both "for better" and "for worse," and expect to stay committed anyway.

Chapter 7

Lessons in How to Leave the Church and End Up Staying

Confession. I haven't always taken Wise Counselor's advice.

Call me a fair-weather friend. A bandwagon Christian. A wishy-washy believer. I have attempted — more than once — to abandon the church. However, as it turns out, I am not particularly successful at running away.

I think I get my talent in this department from my mother. She once told me a story about when she tried to run away as a child. She packed her bags and set off walking. Unfortunately, she wasn't allowed to cross the street without a grown-up, so she had to return home.

Likewise, I sometimes found kindredness among a generation of church runaways — many of whom had grown noticeably tired of mechanized religion but never did end up getting too far from home. I suppose you could liken us to kids who got mad at our parents, packed up our knapsacks, and took off to the tree fort in the backyard.

As we're camping out on the outskirts of the church, many of us are still involved in the church's story. We engage in daily dialogues about faith both in person and via the Internet and social networks. We invest our time in meaningful activities (like community service) that reflect our alignment with Christ's mission. We still live in rich community with our Christian friends, whom we allow to speak authentically into our lives. Although we may not necessarily be in church every week, many of us still consider ourselves unofficial extensions of the church's mission. We kind of want to be affiliated with the church, but we kind of don't. We are indecisive people who have run away from our local congregations only to pitch our tents on the church lawn.

As we try to decide whether to continue to invest in the institutional church, here is my humble suggestion. Before we pack our U-Hauls, forward our mail, and relocate to some distant philosophical peninsula far away from the church, it may be wise to revisit a timeless truth that applies both inside and outside the church. And that is this: *progress isn't painless.*

Great things usually come at a price. Life bears out this principle time and time again. Take birth pains, for instance. I'd yet to attempt childbearing when the first version of this book came out, but I'd watched enough women on the big screen gritting their teeth while hissing "hee-heee-hooooo" to know if my house ever caught fire, the first thing I was saving on my way out the door was my birth control. Now that I've coproduced two beautiful newborn babies, years later, I can credibly verify that these creatures emerge via physical and emotional struggle.

College is often the same way. You can't get on to learning the fun and inspiring stuff until you sit through the painfully tedious prereqs — all of which are conveniently available in three-hour-long night classes. (And somehow, a course in ancient Greek mythology is absolutely necessary to success in any career field.)

I have slowly come to believe that pain is a necessary part of moving forward because it provides the incentive to adopt needed change or growth. Rarely, for instance, do churches make needed changes while what they're doing is working smoothly. Not that the committee members drafting the local church's next five-year plan aren't wild and edgy in their own way. But let's face it, they usually aren't the type to strap the church onto the local fairground's Tilt-A-Whirl and give it a spin just for the rush. Sometimes they need a little pain to push them along.

Minus the pain, church leaders can seem to have this unwritten cardinal rule that we tack on to the end of the Romans Road when no one is looking. *All have sinned and fallen short of the glory of God.... The wages of sin is death, but the gift of God is eternal life through Jesus Christ our Lord.... AND if it isn't broken, don't change it.* Or, as some almost-translations say: *If it isn't shattered into millions of unrecognizable pieces* and *on fire, don't change it.*

Not only are institutions, including churches, often resistant to change, but there is also no handbook to spell out how confronting our weaknesses might play out in a church context. And that makes it scary.

Somewhere in my first year of college, I realized that adult life doesn't always go exactly the way we want it to. As a freshman, I had applied to be a peer adviser for the following year. And yes, a peer adviser sounds like something anyone can do by just dispensing some casual advice to a peer. But this particular position, called a PA, was different because *I was paid*. And in college, money is the sixth love language.

So I interviewed. Tried to convince the hiring panel that if they gave me the job, students would camp out for days and line up around the dorm for miles to hear my guru-on-the-mountaintop-caliber advice.

But you know, the panel was worried about how the lines would block traffic — so they didn't hire me. There I was, a college student who already had a number of burdens — all of which seemed especially paralyzing at the time but just happen to be slipping my mind right now (who wants to bet they had something to do with those particularly troubling creatures called *boys*?) — and Student Development just hauled off and didn't even hire me.

The *nerve* of some people, huh?

And so I quickly entered all my circumstances into my convenient Christian calculator, which immediately spit out the equation: disappointment = college must not be in God's will.

Unfortunately, my dad was surprisingly resistant to my well-conceived plan to immediately quit college and fly off to some remote village — which I would choose by closing my eyes and pointing at a globe — to do relief work of any kind. I thought, *At least the natives will appreciate my leadership!*

I remember being somewhat skeptical as Dad sat across from me at the world's slowest fast-food restaurant and told me that periods of difficulty or pain are not completely accurate indicators that God wants us to abandon our current commitments overnight.

I was not sold on Dad's theory right away, but since there's that one verse about having a long life if you respect your parents, I decided to listen through at least *one* ear.

Then my dad brought up Psalm 23.

And I was thinking, *Tell me he didn't just say Psalm 23 — the infamous Shepherd's Psalm! Does he know how many cotton-ball sheep these hands have made?*

But when your dad is my dad (i.e., someone who can turn a peanut butter and jelly sandwich into an altar call), there is always some wild card you never really counted on.

So my dad says, "You know Psalm 23, right?"

Do I know Psalm 23? Please ... did Noah's kids have chores?

Just for good measure, I began rattling it off in the most bored tone I could muster. "The LORD is my shepherd; I shall not want. He maketh me to lie down in green pastures...." (Um, yeah ... all PKs who are worth their salt know the KJV.)

My dad nodded, satisfied that my third-grade memory verses had stuck. "So where are you when his rod and staff are comforting you?"

Ahh, weren't you listening? I quickly repeat Psalm 23 to myself. "In the valley of the shadow of death?"

"And where is the table where your cup runs over?"

"Um ... [repeating it again] ... in the presence of my enemies?"

Thus ended another course in What They Never Taught You in Sunday School. Apparently, those "hard times" parts of the faith had been there the whole time.

And, apparently, my dad was not the only one in on the conspiracy theory.

Bill Hybels, founding pastor of Willow Creek Community Church, must be in on the secret too. I once heard Hybels acknowledge that staying faithful to the church is sometimes so difficult, all a person can do is "put one foot in front of the other."

In fact, the more I investigate, the more I'm convinced that people have known about the flaws of the faith for *centuries*!

Take Saint John of the Cross, who lived nearly five hundred years before me. John wanted to bring changes to the Carmelite order of monks. But when he voiced his criticisms of the church, they locked him away in a prison cell. While imprisoned, John wrote a series of reflections titled *Dark Night of the Soul*, which describes how periods of pain are integrated into our "normal" rhythms of life. John points out that during painful moments, God is still giving good things, but because life has lost its "felt" sweetness, our eyes filter out the good and we remain in a state of seeming emptiness.

John goes on to note that pain may be a valid part of God's plan, a useful element of Christian experience. Because God is no longer revealing himself through the highs of ordinary human experience, we must struggle with God and our painful circumstances. And in this sometimes intense reflection, God often reveals things in the darkness that we would never stop to examine in the light.

Maybe this is the same process Paul was talking about in Romans 5:3 – 5 when he said, "We also glory in our sufferings, because we know that suffering produces perseverance; perseverance, character; and character, hope. And hope does not put us to shame, because God's love has been poured out into our hearts through the Holy Spirit, who has been given to us."

How's that for mind-boggling? If Paul is right, then suffering is actually linked to the production of hope. In my disillusionment, I often saw suffering or pain as reason to abandon hope. However, I seemed to be applying the verse backward. It doesn't say that frustration is a sign that all hope is lost; it says suffering is actually a necessary ingredient for producing hope!

It's even more mind-blowing when I think about why Paul likely knew this firsthand. It's because of what he observed in the church of his day. Oftentimes, when we think of the first-century church, we idealize it, even glorify it. We shore up our mission statements around a couple of handpicked verses that talk of the early church's Camelot moments.

Acts 2:44 is probably the most referenced of such passages, which of course says, "All the believers were together and had everything in common. They sold property and possessions to give to anyone who had need."

We read this and think, *Yes! This — this sharing of life and possessions, this caring for each other's needs — is what church was meant to be!* And then, in contrast, we become disappointed when our modern-day churches don't function this way, when self-absorption becomes the norm and redistribution of wealth to benefit the needy isn't even on the radar.

But this snapshot of the Acts 2 church is — when cut apart from its context — one of the misleading impressions we may need to abandon, because on further investigation, we see that the Acts 2 church was far from perfect.

In Acts 4 the leaders of the church are arrested. In Acts 5 two church members drop dead on the spot after lying. (I don't know about you, but I think it's safe to say that if two church attendees dropped dead during a church service as punishment for some wrongdoing, I might become disillusioned.) In Acts 6 the church is accused of being racist. In Acts 7 another church leader is stoned to death for heresy. In Acts 9 the church hesitates to welcome Paul, a new convert, into their community because of his past. In Acts 10 the church criticizes Peter for rubbing shoulders with non-Jews. In Acts 15 church leaders argue over whether to make Gentiles follow the Jews' detailed religious customs. Also in Acts 15 there is a personality conflict between church leaders

79

Paul, Barnabas, and John Mark. Paul doesn't want to travel with John Mark because he abandoned them on a previous mission trip. And for the rest of Acts, Paul interacts with churches around the region that have lots of drama and a lengthy list of issues to sort through.

Church, even for the Acts 2 community, seemed to be this paradoxical mix of goods and bads, warmth and challenge, unity and tension.

But you know who I don't think would have been surprised by all this? By our disillusionment? By the paradoxical nature of Psalm 23? By the experience of Saint John of the Cross? Or Paul? Or the Acts 2 community?

Jesus.

The first time the word *church* is recorded in the Bible, in Matthew 16:18, it is spoken by Jesus: "And I tell you that you are Peter, and on this rock I will build my church, and the gates of Hades [or hell] will not overcome it."

I don't know about you, but I am beginning to think it was no accident that the very first time Jesus mentioned the church, he declared that the forces of evil would not overcome it. Jesus knew that the church was going to have a hard road ahead of it, that the church might sometimes look like it was going under. It seems that he was anticipating our panic, our feelings of defeat, and our disillusionment in how he unpacked this message for his followers. *There's this thing called church, and by the way, the forces of evil aren't going to prevail against it.*

In light of this knowledge, I've slowly grown to suspect that the dark moments define the Christian faith, and its church, just as much *or more* than the bright ones. If this is true, then Bill Hybels's definition of faithfulness, "putting one foot in front of the other," seems like one of the most realistic ones. And I'm glad Hybels said it this way too. I have a feeling that my generation needs such grounded, unairbrushed definitions of faith.

We may sometimes feel like running away from the church. More than once. And we may even run away. More than once. But our faithfulness may be resolving that somehow, some way, we will keep coming back.

DISCUSSION QUESTIONS

1. The author describes herself and some of her generation as runaways to the tree fort in the church's backyard. Have you ever run away to such a ridiculously close place? Explain.

2. Why do you think we expect progress to happen without pain?

3. Have you ever really thought about the apparent pain evidenced in the Shepherd's Psalm? Why do you think we tend to focus on the good parts of this passage rather than the tough ones?

4. What other Scriptures or lessons from church tradition suggest that progress is not painless? Try to think of other Old or New Testament stories that reinforce the author's list of imperfect church experiences drawn from the book of Acts.

5. Think through the words of Romans 5:3 – 5. Has suffering in your life ever produced hope? Share what this experience was like.

KEY IDEAS

◆ When we expect progress to be painless and easy, we set ourselves up for disappointment.

◆ Both life and the Bible, particularly the book of Acts, paint a picture of faith life that is far from perfect.

◆ When we picture comforting psalms like Psalm 23, we often focus on the image of Jesus as a comforting shepherd walking with us through a lush green meadow near a sparkling brook. But what the chapter actually conveys is that he is there beside us, with his staff, when we are in the valley of the shadow of death or at the table in the presence of our enemies.

◆ Even though many of us may be quick to assume our suffering is a sign that there is no hope, Paul actually said that suffering helps produce hope.

◆ Our definition of faithfulness in hard times may be less heroic than some often-heralded biblical figures who slayed giants or survived lions' dens. It may just look like putting one foot in front of the other.

◆ It is often when we push through the darkness that we see opportunities to grow and improve that we never would have seen in the light.

Chapter 8

How Can
We Go On Living?

For some of us, there may come a moment, after healing from a particular bout of disappointment, when we begin to think we are not so fragile as to have our lives or faith derailed by such deep disappointment again.

After walking through the stages described earlier — realizing we're not alone, identifying what disillusions us, letting our negative emotions go, separating our identities from our bad experiences, learning to see disillusionment as an opportunity, and adjusting our expectations — we may begin to feel as though we've moved beyond most of our previous frustrations and discovered ways to live toward solutions that will help repair the deficits we see in the church. And along with that, we may feel as though we've developed especially thick, almost impenetrable skin.

It may be hard to believe now, but someday we may begin to think about disillusionment as an experience that happened a long time ago, *before* we grew so significantly and started to see the world through a more mature lens. When this happens, we may be relieved to feel we're operating as normal again. While we may not voice it aloud, subconsciously at least, we may think the real cause for alarm has passed. We think the storm is over, that it is safe to settle into run-of-the-mill ministry oblivion and casually live our identity as church once more.

We hope so. But probably not, right?

In an earlier chapter, I compared disillusionment to a chronic illness because it has the ability to resurface out of nowhere. I said that because that's what happened to me. I worked through a lot of my pain over some of the bad that unraveled in my faith communities. I learned how to appropriately represent my concerns about how the church — the historic, global version — functioned. I found the confidence to acknowledge and challenge instances from history and modern-day society where Christians seemed to misrepresent Christ's message. I learned to grow up and buck up and correct some of the ways I misrepresented Christ myself. All the while, I developed better research skills and an improved ability to articulate biblical and rational arguments to support my positions. And with help, I found some solutions that I was excited to invest in *for life*.

As a result, I thought I had shaken free of most of my former frustrations. If you would have asked me, I would have sighed in relief and told you that, thankfully, I had officially put my disillusionment to rest. Unfortunately, however, life is not always what it seems. If something bad enough happens, all those former anxieties and frustrations can be triggered by some automated mental process and restored to new life before you even realize what is happening.

The second time I found myself experiencing deep disillusionment, my distress was not just related to the global church's interactions with marginalized people or even my own city's responses to those in need. It was not a distant disillusionment with a nameless, faceless church "system," and its victims were not groups of only recently discovered strangers. This time I encountered disillusionment in Christian communities that had names. And faces. In fact, a lot of faces. The names weren't just any names and the faces weren't just any faces either. This time the church bore familiar names — names that were entirely precious to me, names that I had strongly identified with, names that had come to represent so much that was good in the faith arena and in myself. The faces were the faces of people I dearly loved.

In two back-to-back instances in my life, people I related to, people who inspired me, people I *loved* were caught up in messy, hurtful church-related stories that awakened a new kind of grief in me. Combined with my previous disillusionment — which now seemed even more valid than before — this fresh disappointment tragically skewed my perception of the church in ways I still haven't fully recovered from.

Suddenly, Christian community again became synonymous with pain. Walking into a church building — any church building — felt like getting repeatedly punched in the stomach until my body finally went into welcome shock and I became so numb that I didn't even care that I was being punched.

Ghosts from the past haunted my memories, ruining potentially positive experiences in the present. Ghosts from the future repressed my ability to dream, constantly reminding me that any vision — no matter how God-inspired, no matter what the level of commitment or talent — could fall apart at the seams as if it had never existed.

One particular night, I began sobbing. Similar to my life flashing before my eyes, my mind replayed all the people — those I was personally connected to, those on the other side of the world, those from the pages of the history books — who had paid some sort of cost while involved in the work of the church. And I just could not stop crying. When my husband came in to investigate, I was unusually uncommunicative. All I remember repeating — over and over again — is, "It's too hard. It's just too hard." I felt as though I had spent my entire young adult life living for an institution that wasn't worth living for. And now that my former optimism about church was shattered, I didn't know what causes — if any — remained worthy of my ongoing life investment.

You can perhaps best hear my renewed conflict about my involvement in the church by reading a blog post I wrote at the time.

08.17.04

I am frequently torn between two perspectives. On one hand, I earnestly want to invest my life in the global church. I want to live with a sense of expectation that God will complete each vision he started ... in my life and elsewhere.

Even in the midst of grief and tension, I want to speak from a deeply rooted, unwavering sense of hope.

The other part of me, however, wants to wave the white flag of sad acknowledgment. I want to give up the cause and admit that — no matter what I do — I cannot change the painful potential of my world.

I want to concede the irony of it all ... that if I wish to pursue God's kingdom here, I must step into the line of fire. If I want to help take the hill, I will have to watch my friends fall beside me and be wounded myself.

And despite all my ambition, I too will fail to fully carry out my good intentions. It seems we cannot pursue the good without tasting the bad. It rains on the just and unjust alike. "Frankly, this side of eternity we will never unravel the good from the bad, the pure from the impure," Richard Foster says. But he points out, "God is big enough to receive us with all our mixture. That is what grace means, and not only are we saved by it, we live by it as well."[9]

During the height of my disillusionment, following a morning worship service at the church where I had formerly worked, I fell into seemingly casual conversation with the wife of one of our church's elders. Along with her husband, she had been attending our church over half my lifetime — a commitment that, by itself, gave them credibility in my eyes.

Perhaps what I respect most about this couple is that when I spoke with them about my own painful wrestling matches with the church at large, they did not try to casually explain away my concerns. They were honest. Their experience with the global church had also been marked with bouts of hurtful disillusionment. On a couple of occasions, in fact, this disillusionment had severely diminished the wife's desire to attend or participate in local church community.

In one dark moment, when the weight of my concerns seemed particularly heavy, I posed this question to the elder's wife through tears: "If the church is the hope of the world, then why would I go on hoping?" (I can be a bit theatrical sometimes, if you haven't noticed.)

She smiled sadly. "Sarah," she said, "don't let anyone mislead you. Sometimes leaders claim that the church is the hope of the world in an effort to help people understand their shared identity in Christ's mission. But the church is *not* the hope of the world. Jesus is."

And, of course, she was right.

Sometimes I think we must have read the Bible and our Marvel comic book back-to-back and emerged with the impression that we are supposed to be superheroes who right all the world's wrongs. Somewhere along the line, I had gradually bought into this logical fallacy. In my attempts to examine how I felt church *should be*, I had allowed too much of my faith to hinge on the humans who drove the institution. But the Great Commission was not passed out with spandex suits or vinyl capes. And that, of course, is because we aren't the hope of the world. For Pete's sake, on our own we're not even the hope of Metropolis.

Through this woman's counsel and the following months of reflection, I found the answer that closed the gap between what church is and what I believed church should be. His name is Jesus. Jesus is the matrix that makes it possible to see my world, and even my flawed religious institutions, in light of hope.

We Christians were never the hope. Yes, we were and are carriers of the hope. But we ourselves are only reflections — often dim reflections — of the hope we internalize: Jesus Christ. Obviously, the church is *the* key earthly player in Christ's unfolding drama. But when we get carried away with our own role, we risk inflating our true position.

In effect, as Paul describes it in Colossians 2:18 – 19, we run around like a church that's lost its head: "[People who delight in false humility go] into great detail about what they have seen; they are puffed up with idle notions by their unspiritual mind. They have lost connection with the head, from whom the whole body, supported and held together by its ligaments and sinews, grows as God causes it to grow."

But I can't be unduly hard on the current-day Christian institutions. We certainly are not the first to fail to live out our correct identity in the history of the church. Unfortunately, the pages of the Bible are littered with examples of people who edited the roles God gave them to suit their own desires. This pattern is especially evident in the life of God's people during the time of the major prophets. Jeremiah, for example, shows us that. Judah was being threatened by Babylon, but the nation didn't respond with the urgency such a threat should generate. Rather than realign their allegiance to God, their true hope, they seemed to place their trust in a genetic insurance policy. *Because we're God's chosen people, we obviously can't be wiped out.*

But Jeremiah had a message for Judah, which in essence could be summarized, "Wanna bet?" Jeremiah urged Judah not to rest in a false sense of security, thinking they were safe because *they* were the inheritors of true religion and the guardians of the temple. On the contrary, Jeremiah insisted, they needed to internalize God's truth to have any real claim to hope.

With Jeremiah as background, it is Ezekiel who clinches the lesson for me. And this time, God's followers — who were now relying on what they deemed to be a hopeful combination of idol and sun worship — had brought their sins into the place of worship (Ezekiel 8). They were literally keeping idols in secret rooms within the temple!

The Old Testament depiction of God's response may seem a bit surprising. He summoned six warriors to slay everyone, including women and small children, who failed to rely on him. Then he went one step further. He commanded the warriors to defile the temple by piling the city's dead bodies in its courts (which would have been a monstrous grievance according to laws concerning temple cleanliness). What followed was the deepest wound of Judah's judgment: God removed his glory from the temple.

I wonder, ideally, how should Judah have responded to the message of the prophets?

Certainly, to revert to a hope founded in God and his ways would have been in order. But I also wonder, was God hoping that even one priest would pull a Paul Revere ride, shouting, "We are misled! We do not glean our hope from our building!"? I like to think that someone with more guts, and a little bit of irreverence, might have even cried out, "And let the sin-stained temple burn, God, because we know we don't need the temple. The temple is nothing, God. Our real hope is you."

And I can't help wondering (and I truly am just wondering, not instructing), is it possible that, at times, God has acted or will act similarly toward later groupings of his people? Do we, like Israel, sometimes misunderstand our identity, believing that the institutional church — the collection of buildings, the mechanized systems, the lists of intellectual assents — is the source of our hope?

To be honest, I hear a lot of Israel in myself. When I asked our elder's wife, "If the church is the hope of the world, then why would I go on hoping?" my attitude was not a far cry from Israel's reaction when they realized their temple had fallen. When they see the dead bodies in the courtyard in Ezekiel 33:10, Israel despairs: "Our offenses and sins weigh us down, and we are wasting away because of them. How then can we live?"

This, too, is what I wanted to know. *If the current church's offenses and sins weigh us down, and we are wasting away because of them, how then can we live?*

And this is where we are relieved to remember our hope lies safely outside of ourselves and our religious institutions. It lies beyond the broken church in God's response to Israel's cry, and to mine.

"How then can we live?" Israel asks.

"As I live," says the Lord.

We don't sustain ourselves, in other words. He sustains us.

In tracking these ideas, I sense that there may be a connection between our disillusionment and how we sometimes mistakenly see ourselves. Perhaps it is when we market ourselves as the hope of the world, or when we believe other humans hold the hope of the world for us, without proper acknowledgment of God and Christ as our source, that we foster disillusionment. But it is not our own ability to function perfectly that sustains our ministry efforts.

How do we emerge from the darkness and renew our identity as God's church? How do we go on living?

"As I live," says the Lord.

We don't sustain ourselves; we're sustained by him.

DISCUSSION QUESTIONS

1. Have you ever thought that you shook disillusionment only to have it return? What happened?
2. Have you ever fallen into the trap that the author describes by drawing hope from the humans who run the church?
3. Have you experienced a moment in your church or faith history when you literally wondered, *How am I supposed to go on?* Describe it.

4. Do you agree with the author that sometimes we place disproportionate importance on buildings and systems and forget that our salvation does not lie in the temple or brick-and-mortar church but in Christ? If so, why do you think this happens?

KEY IDEAS

◆ Sometimes we think we have overcome disillusionment, that we are past that stage. But life will always include new instances of disappointment and suffering.

◆ In our severest frustrations, we may want to throw up our hands and ask ourselves, "How can I go on living?" The answer is that we do not sustain ourselves; God sustains us.

◆ As we try to train church leaders to carry God's hope to the world, we often use lines like "The church is the hope of the world" to inspire and encourage people of faith to remember the importance of the mission. But this can be misleading because the church is not the hope of the world; Jesus is.

Chapter 9

Withness

Should I stay committed to my local church even if it seems to overlook or dismiss some of the values of Christ I hold dearest? And if I choose to stay, will I be missing out on a better fit elsewhere or, even worse, will I be ignoring better opportunities to influence my generation?

These questions, which are common to those who are frustrated with their churches, arose as my friends and I read Philippians one evening (see 2:1–2). In this passage, Paul called for unity in the church at Philippi, but we wondered aloud how his words should transfer to our time and geography. It seemed good and right and consistent with overarching biblical themes for Christians of any era to be, as Paul said, "like-minded, having the same love, being one in spirit and of one mind."

But we still had questions.

"Does that mean we're stuck where we are? Trapped being *unified* with the same local church as long as we live in this area?" someone asked.

The rest of us shrugged, hoping *church* would never be a synonym for life imprisonment.

"But if your church doesn't live out their on-paper beliefs, don't you think you are justified in trying to find a church that will?" another countered.

"Or do you think we're supposed to stick with the church and help them reach the people they are missing?"

Other times, we think we spot loopholes in Paul's writings.

"Technically, can't we be unified with a church *in spirit and purpose* without actually physically attending it?"

"Or can we start our own church and just be unified with ourselves?" another person said with a laugh.

"But if we live by that rule, won't our own kids one day abandon us to start their own church?"

"Would it be such a bad thing if they did?"

(By the way, my friends and I decided it would be. We like intergenerational church.)

We know we are not the first to ask these questions. But the church's history doesn't make it any easier to discern how this ancient encouragement might apply to us. In fact, it almost seems to make the question all the more difficult.

Almost everyone in the institutional church seems to think highly of Martin Luther, for example. He is widely respected for challenging the flawed religious systems of his day. But we seem to skip over the underlying catch in giving Luther our admiration: Didn't Luther's efforts eventually encourage his generation to shift their energies away from the church of their day?

As Tim Stafford, senior writer at *Christianity Today*, has pointed out, "Until Martin Luther, the church was the immovable center of gravity." Moreover, "Luther never intended to move that center of gravity. He wanted to purify the church, not defy its authority. Nevertheless, his protests led to schism."[10]

I must confess that the "reformer" in some of us isn't convinced Luther would have made the strides he did had he not distanced himself from the church of his upbringing. But was he right to inspire a separate movement to try to correct the existing church's flaws? Or should Luther have spent his remaining years patiently praying toward unity with a church who didn't see it his way?

To make matters more complex, Luther isn't the only example who makes leaving churches seem like a viable solution. Religious history, in fact, is marked by case after case of disagreements and schisms, usually over how to interpret various Scriptures. From the get-go, even first-century church leaders like Peter and James seemed to view themselves as reformers of Judaism. They maintained belief in Jesus as Messiah but, at the same time, continued to follow many traditional Jewish laws.

Their awkward footing in both camps made for tension more than once.

Another point of contrast arose over the shared ritual of baptism. The apostle Paul — who wasn't one of the twelve disciples — apparently saw baptism differently than the disciple John. Paul called his version "baptism in the Spirit" while naming John's version "a baptism of repentance." And when the people John had baptized said they hadn't even heard about the Holy Spirit, Paul baptized them again. Even then, while the eyewitnesses of Jesus were still alive, there were apparently different takes on the best way to do things.

The Roman Empire eventually recognized Pauline Christianity as its official religion. And in this era, all Christians were still considered part of the one, holy catholic (meaning universal) and apostolic church, who largely expressed their faith through missionary and charity work. Sure, disgruntled in-fighting existed. But wayward factions considered heretics were few and far between, having little to no influence on Christianity's early trajectory.

Ahh, those were the days — the "church is sometimes disgruntled but still in one piece" glory days.

By the third century, new ideas appeared on the Christian horizon. For example, the monastic life — which focused on abandoning the pleasures of this world — evolved from the Christian beliefs of Saint Anthony and his followers in Egypt. And this strand of believers expressed their faith differently, not through traveling evangelism but through personal meditation and practices.

The variations continued. But in 1054, the growing differences over hierarchy led the church to a breaking point. The bishops of Rome had tried to claim rule in the East, but the East wasn't having it. Unable to agree, a group that came to be recognized as the Eastern Orthodox Church split from the Roman Catholics.

The church got by a few hundred more years, primarily split in two pieces until the infamous Luther and the Reformers came in. This group protested at how church officials inserted themselves between God and his followers, refusing to honor an individual's right to interpret the Scriptures for himself. The Reformers were also outraged that Catholics had adopted what they considered to be non-biblical practices such as the selling of indulgences. This set the next major division in motion, in which a group known as Protestants (i.e., "protestors") split off from the Catholic Church.

This, it turned out, was an even more poignant break, one that fractured the Roman Catholics' relationship with a variety of groups. In essence, it was the first stone in an avalanche. As the Reformation spirit spread, it birthed other denominations. One, of course, was Lutheranism, which later broke into multiple strands, including today's Missouri Synod and Evangelical Lutheran Church in America.

As Switzerland was swept into the reforms, even more denominations were born. This time, largely influenced by John Calvin, the Presbyterian denomination and the Reformed Church came into being. During this same general time frame, Switzerland also birthed the Anabaptists, who were the predecessors of today's Amish, Mennonites, Quakers, and Baptists who broke off from them.

In 1534 major church division was still in the headlines. England's King Henry VIII broke away from the authority of the pope and formed the Anglican Church. When people with Anglican ties moved to America, the movement became known as Episcopalianism, which like the others also further broke off into multiple strands. Some of those who sought to reform the Anglican Church were called Methodists, championed by John Wesley. More than forty denominations descended from the Methodist movement, including, of course, United Methodists, Free Methodists, and Wesleyans.

Now, according to the Center for the Study of Global Christianity, there are approximately 41,000 Christian denominations and organizations in the world.[11]

Hearing about these people who struck out before us to reinvent their churches may inspire some of us. It may grieve some of us too. But in any case, reform efforts are nothing new. Because of that, it may be wise to stockpile some grace for those who want to reimagine the churches of today. Whether we like it or not, our own style of church probably came out of some previous generation's attempt to reform the church of their day. And those who call for reform today aren't reforming some original expression of the church. They're reforming the version that came out of the last reform.

In light of this history, then, what principles should guide those experiencing disillusionment? Under what circumstances and to what extent are we to seek unity with existing local churches? And under what circumstances do we move forward, like many of those before us, with new church plants and movements as reminders of God's fresh involvement with his church?

We're back to asking the question posed by the popular song by the Clash: "Should I stay or should I go?" Before we delve into this question more deeply, though, I'd like to offer an idea, one that proved helpful to me no matter how I chose to involve or affiliate myself with churches. And that is this: whatever your situation — whether you're disillusioned with a pastor, a local church, a denomination, the concept of church, whatever — strive to practice as much "withness" as you can. By this I mean wherever you end up, keep finding reasons to spend time *with* and have conversation *with* people whose expressions of Christianity make you uncomfortable.

Acknowledging that life has limits, try as much as you can, wherever you can, for as long as you can to maintain relationship, and even kindredness, familialness, with other people of faith in your life.

While this is not always easy to do, the following are some observations I've made that have helped me practice withness in my scenario.

Observation 1: Our frustrations are not wholly new or unique, and we join a timeless band of people who've experienced disillusionment with the church.

The first time I was pregnant, my dad made an off-the-cuff

comment that stuck with me. I was talking about the overwhelming amount of advice concerning infant development, early sleep patterns, immunization, prenatal diet, and so on available in books and on websites for first-time moms.

"Well, it's good to be informed," Dad noted, "but also keep in mind that a lot of people, like tribal groups, for example, don't have access to all these opinions. And they still somehow manage to give birth and raise children and repopulate their villages."

Ahhh. Balance.

Granted, we might not want to exchange our health or food resources with some tribal peoples. But yes, generations of women from all different geographies have been birthing children into this world without following every last tip in the latest, most up-to-date volume of *What to Expect When You're Expecting.*

My mind quickly traveled to the urban teens I worked with each day, many of whom became parents far earlier and with far fewer resources than I would consider ideal. And their children, too, were clothed and fed and breathing.

Release the panic button. I'll probably make it too.

Sometimes, the way I panic and settle into peace about church is no different. I have to take a deep breath and acknowledge, *I am not the first person to be disillusioned with Christianity, and I won't be the last. I follow in the footsteps of a long line of humans who struggled with the intersection of faith and life before me.*

This reminds me that even though it's hard, most people make it. They survive the struggle and the difficult emotions. They muddle through. And it kindly suggests to me that I too will probably find my way.

Observation 2: Regardless of our opinions, we can stand against actions that result in isolation.

Usually when my faith and pain collided, fight or flight kicked in. I felt torn. I wanted to stay in church but at the same time wanted to leave. I wanted to cut ties as soon as possible, but I also wanted to stay connected forever. With no clarity, I thumbed through the truths of the past. I went back ages, to the ancients, to what was known from oral traditions, from the intentions of God passed down through creation narratives even before the books of Law were committed to scroll. This is what I discovered: *God does not want us to be alone.* And I resolved, even in my disoriented state, to try to align myself with this desire God had for us whenever I could.

I try not to strike out on my own, to abandon the wisdom of people of faith who have gone before me, or to sever myself from our current-day faith communities, because that would be to choose isolation, to opt for aloneness — the opposite of what God wants.

Along those same lines, I resist ending relationships with those who follow Jesus but hold a different opinion than me on a given verse or tradition. To do this is to force aloneness on them. It brings about an end result that goes against God's desire that we live in community, which is a principle I see consistently threaded through Scripture from Genesis to the epistles.

I fear that we forget this part of God's instructions for us sometimes. We abuse our power to cause or endorse aloneness. We too easily distance ourselves from our critics, citing what we claim are permission-giving passages like Matthew 18:15 – 17, which tells us if a brother or sister who sins fails to listen to our reproof, we are to "treat them as you would a pagan or a tax collector."

On that front, I'm not always buying what we're selling. I'm not sure Matthew 18 was meant to justify severing relationships. I think an equally strong argument could be made that the intent of the passage is to purposefully make it difficult to justify disconnection. Take the three vignettes leading up to this often-cited passage and the one that follows it.

First, Jesus was in Capernaum when the disciples began arguing over who would be considered the greatest in heaven. Jesus seemed to think it was the wrong question altogether, for he didn't even entertain it. He just called a child over and said that the greatest are those who take the humble position of a child (Matthew 18:1–5). The theme at play here seems to be: *Don't try to outdo others; humble yourself.*

In the next scene, as he did a few other times in Scripture, Jesus focused his listeners away from judging others and toward self-examination. He didn't say go and examine other people and try to remove *their* sin, but cut off anything that causes *you* to stumble (Matthew 18:6–9).

Third, following this story, Jesus told his hearers that even with ninety-nine out of a hundred sheep safely in the fold, he would leave the ninety-nine out on the hill to fend for themselves so he could go after the one who was lost (Matthew 18:10–14). He was saying, "I'm not looking to judge the one who is lost; I'm going to ditch the rest of you to go save him."

This is when Jesus said the famous words of Matthew 18:15–17. If a person is sinning (missing the mark, straying from rightness or honor), go tell him. If he doesn't listen, bring a couple of witnesses. If he still doesn't listen, take it before the whole community and send him on his way.

What's curious about this process, when I imagine how it would most likely unfold, is that it provides a natural safeguard for both parties, the accuser and the accused. If someone is poison, and the community collectively recognizes the harm the person brings, they remove the source of threat. But, on the other hand, it contains a safety net in the event that the accuser is simply angry at someone he disagrees with and would like to oust the person from the church over a difference of opinion or as a matter of personal vengeance. Maybe an unfair accuser gets two or three friends to agree to expel their antagonist. But they take their case before the whole church community and someone says, "Wait a minute. I don't think this is the sort of thing we should be excommunicating people for." And the ousting agenda gets shelved.

The community, at least in some cases, protects both parties from harm.

Finally, Jesus follows up his teaching with the parable of the unmerciful servant who refuses to forgive a small debt even though he has had his own larger debt forgiven. Jesus ends the parable in verse 35 by saying, "This is how my heavenly Father will treat each of you unless you forgive your brother or sister from your heart." This message isn't arguable: Jesus says, "You're forgiven, so don't let me catch you not forgiving others."

So here's what I see when I review all these stories thematically:

Who's the greatest? *Humble yourself like a child.*

Cut off anything that causes you to stumble. *Examine yourself.*

Jesus would leave the ninety-nine to go after the one. *I'm not condemning the lost one; I'm leaving you to save him.*

If you disagree about sin, take it to the whole church community and oust any source of harm.

The unmerciful servant failed to forgive a debt. *Don't let me catch you not forgiving when you've been forgiven.*

While severing relationship à la Matthew 18 could certainly be beneficial in some circumstances, I don't neccessarily think the chapter intended for us to adopt this action as the first line of defense or as the norm. To me, Jesus' teaching here seems to have a bottom line like a question on a final exam where we students are asked, "True or false: the thesis — or the statement that best describes the meaning of the passage — is 'Oust anyone who sins from the church.'"

A less quoted verse, in my experience, is found in 2 Corinthians. I remember, as a child, when I first stumbled upon it, because it absolutely dumbfounded me that Matthew 18 had become such a popular go-to passage for confrontation and I'd never ever heard this one dropped into conversation.

This is Paul talking:

If anyone has caused grief, he has not so much grieved me as he has grieved all of you to some extent — not to put it too severely. The punishment inflicted on him by the majority is sufficient. Now instead, you ought to forgive and comfort him, so that he will not be overwhelmed by excessive sorrow. I urge you, therefore, to reaffirm your love for him. Another reason I wrote you was to see if you would stand the test and be obedient in everything. Anyone you forgive, I also forgive. And what I have forgiven — if there was anything to forgive — I have forgiven in the sight of Christ for your sake, in order that Satan might not outwit us. For we are not unaware of his schemes. (2 Corinthians 2:5 – 11)

Now, some protectors of the church, I know, might be concerned by what I'm advocating here. *But wait! What if the person is really, really sinning? Like straight up defying the ways of God?*

Well then, as Matthew 18 says, you are justified in treating that person like a pagan or tax collector.

And how do you treat a pagan or tax collector?

You eat with them so much people start to gossip about you, you turn the other cheek, you go the extra mile, you give them your coat and cloak too. You love your enemies. You pray for those who persecute you. You judge only as you want to be judged. You worry about the log in your own eye more than you do the speck in someone else's. And if these pagans whip you and beat you and nail you to a cross, you look to God and say, "God, forgive them, they don't fully understand what they're doing."

(Granted, it's easier said than done, eh?)

Another way of standing against isolation, in tension, is — as stated earlier — to make bold and purposeful moves to be "with" others.

Clearly from his presentation as Emmanuel (God with us) in his incarnation as a human, Jesus acted as a mediator who helped people draw near to God rather than become more separate from him. One way he did this was by spending time with the people of his day. And not just one type of person, but every kind of person who lived within the areas he visited.

If you do a cursory flip through the Gospels, you'll find that Jesus chose to spend time with *all* people — even those opposed to him and to each other. The diverse people groups Jesus interacted with included, but were not limited to, men, women, children, shepherds, wise men from foreign countries, fishermen, synagogue officials, the diseased, the demon-possessed, those prone to seizures, the paralyzed, lepers, centurions, the blind, the mute, zealots, Pharisees, Sadducees, hometown citizens, teachers of the law, physicians, tax collectors, the rich, the chief priests, soldiers, governors, thieves, widows, prostitutes, beggars, kings, wedding guests, public officials, Jews, Canaanites, Samaritans, and Syrophoenicians.[12] People didn't have to believe perfectly to belong.

Never, when Jesus was hanging out with his followers, did he require that someone comprehend or even live out everything he was teaching immediately. When the disciples missed their cues again and again, puzzling over metaphors, fighting over position, trying to send children away, missing the point of parables, denying him, and failing to *expect* he would rise from the dead despite his clear assertions that he would, Jesus didn't drop any hammers. He never seemed to pause and assess whether they were the kind of people he should be teamed with. He didn't stop and ask them to explain to him their detailed theological positions on a list of doctrines to see if they were worthy of belonging among his followers. Instead, he seemed resolved that in their belief, they were moving in the right direction and they'd get there in time.

We don't have to interpret frustration as a sign that someone is against us. Emotional involvement may suggest that person is actually deeply aligned with us.

When I was in high school, the JV basketball coach — who was also the winningest softball coach in our school's history — was known to be demanding. On at least one occasion during my freshman year, he threw our entire team out of the gym because we failed to demonstrate the kind of focus he expected.

I remember I went home mad.

But then something happened shortly after that day that I've never forgotten. In the middle of practice, he pulled me aside and said, "Sarah, do you know why I yell at you?" I shook my head no, which seemed better than calling him an angry tyrant. "I get all worked up at you because I believe in you. Not every girl who comes out for sports is going to be here next year or the year after that. But I yell at you because I think you're worth the energy."

It's tempting for church people to see anyone who voices cynicism or calls for change as an enemy. To project onto them some sort of evil motive, rather than to hear the alternatives — confusion, vision, or even, like my coach, *investedness.*

Some people never invest in the church at all. They don't even know what it is like to love a local church community, a denomination, a way of living faith. And others who do know this depth of involvement still don't always bother to try to resolve their concerns. Some of them just walk away without saying a word, never to be heard from again.

It's very possible, then, that the people experiencing fierce emotion about the state of the church are the ones most invested in the church for the long run. They believe in it. They are convinced it can and should do better. They may be on your side more than many of the people who trek alongside you in displays of superficial allegiance. While we may not always be able to align ourselves with those in tension or those who seek reforms, we may be able to find some sort of broader teaming with them in the larger scheme of our Christian mission.

I am reminded how the disciples came to Jesus asking him to disclaim some nondisciples who were doing work in his name. "Teacher," said John, "we saw someone driving out demons in your name and we told him to stop, because he was not one of us."

You probably remember Jesus' response: "Do not stop him.

For no one who does a miracle in my name can in the next moment say anything bad about me, for whoever is not against us is for us" (Mark 9:38 – 40).

It strikes me in both this statement, and in several gospel narratives, that Jesus consistently offered belonging to people whom religious leaders may not have expected him to accept. And it's also interesting to note that it was the Pharisees and sometimes the zealous and uninformed disciples who, in their legalism, were most often trying to exclude others and establish their own superiority.

Even if we judge someone's perspective to be errant or harmful, there is humility in acknowledging that their efforts may still bring about good we would not anticipate. Paul, for example, described how human teachers and philosophers failed to capture the real truths of this world, but how in spite of that, "God was pleased through the foolishness of what was preached to save those who believe" (1 Corinthians 1:21). Perhaps Paul was able to identify how foolishness could be used by God so easily because he himself had once been mistaken in his teachings. He started out as a religious zealot, after all, following God but killing Christians in his name. Yet even after he converted and became a leader, others in the church seem to regularly take issue with him. In 1 Corinthians 9 and 2 Corinthians 11, for example, it appears other leaders in Corinth had a problem with Paul not making his living from the church. It also seems, based on 2 Corinthians 1:15 – 2:4, that Paul was being criticized for not keeping his word to visit the Christians in Corinth. And on another odd occasion, in Philippians 1:15 – 17, other preachers seemed to rise up to take advantage of Paul's imprisonment and preach the gospel for less than noble reasons. Perhaps the most commonly known disagreement involving

Paul, though, is the one found in Acts 15 which describes how Barnabas disagreed with Paul about whether John Mark should be part of their missionary journeys. While some followers of Christ might have taken issue with Paul or competed against him at various times, we can be glad the early church as a whole didn't sever relationship with him in any of these instances since he went on to write half the New Testament.

Willingness to maintain relationship with those who disagree with us and acknowledge that God can still use them can often be difficult, for we humans tend to be impatient, defensive, and concerned with establishing ourselves as right. Perhaps we want to insist the errant teachers who claim the name of Christ in our midst are more volatile and dangerous than Paul or those of his day, that they more grievously betray God and his purposes. Yet when I start to feel judgment boil in my veins, I'm often reminded of our Lord's response to Peter. After Peter betrayed Jesus, whom he knew in person, he went on to be the most prominent leader of the first church.

To me it seems especially logical to err on the side of graciousness, because given the number of verses that we're trying to understand and apply, there's a pretty good chance that the person misapplying a Scripture in some given moment is me.

When we're unsure of or threatened by the positions or motives of our detractors, one possible response is to surrender those concerns to God. I love the balance in the words of Gamaliel, found in Acts 5. On the day in question, a group of jealous Jewish leaders, who were trying to defend the Jewish faith from Christianity's influence, arrested the apostles. The disciples were brought before the Sanhedrin, the assembly of elders, of whom Gamaliel was a member. The case on the floor went like this: The Jewish officials had told the Christians to stop preaching about Jesus, but the Christians had continued, stating they must obey God rather than men. This made the Jewish officials so furious that verse 33 tells us they lobbied to put the Christians to death.

Then entered Gamaliel, a teacher of the Jewish law, and not just any teacher, but a teacher "who was honored by all the people" (v. 34).

"Men of Israel," Gamaliel said, "consider carefully what you intend to do to these men." He reminded the officials about the time they had killed another teacher, Theudas, and how all Theudas's followers were dispersed and nothing ever came of his ideas. "Therefore, in the present case I advise you: Leave these men alone! Let them go! For if their purpose or activity is of human origin, it will fail. But if it is from God, you will not be able to stop these men; you will only find yourselves fighting against God" (Acts 5:35–39).

Good old Gamaliel. He was among the elders of his day, but he retained a humility many of us struggle to match. He retained the ability to let God determine the outcome of those who claimed to teach about him. I don't know about you, but I think we could use a few more Gamaliels in the church today.

DISCUSSION QUESTIONS

1. Can you relate to the conversation the author had with her friends in which they wondered about whether "keeping unity" with other believers could only mean they should stay committed to the same church for life? Have you ever felt torn between leaving and staying in a local church?

2. Prior to reading this book, had you learned about any of the Reformers or past Christian leaders who brought changes to the way society practiced faith? Did any of them inspire you?

3. This chapter recommended practicing "withness" whenever possible. Regardless of whether you stayed or left your current local church or ministry, whom in your life do you feel it would be important to work hard to maintain relationship with over the long term?

4. When have you seen church or faith-related problems result in broken relationships? Why do you think people of faith often resort to disconnecting from those they disagree with?

5. What are some ways you sometimes find yourself disagreeing with other believers? At the same time, what are some areas where you could find agreement and unity with those same people you disagree with?

6. What did you think of the author's opinion about Matthew 18? Did you agree that the main theme of the passage is to encourage humility and relationship rather than disconnection? Or do you disagree? Explain.

7. What did you think of Gamaliel's response? Could his logic be applied to current-day disagreements in church communities? Why or why not?

KEY IDEAS

◆ Ideally we are directed to strive for unity whenever possible. That may mean exercising patience to continue on where we are or maintaining a spirit of unity if we come to believe our work is better suited in a new church community other than the one where we started.

♦ If you have a vision for a healthier or fresh way of living as church, you are in good company. Church history is marked by reformers who sought to bring about change to the belief systems and churches of their generations.

♦ Whether a person decides to stay in their local church or move on, it may be wise to practice as much "withness" as possible. This means acknowledging that life has limits, trying as much as you can wherever you can for as long as you can to maintain relationship with other people of faith in your life.

♦ We are wise to acknowledge that we are not the first to find fault in the church or the first to seek to reform it, but that we are one of many generations who have tried to figure out the best faith models for their eras. We can gain wisdom by learning from those who went before us.

♦ Regardless of our opinions, we can stand against actions that result in isolation.

♦ We can uphold the spirit of the incarnation by being with people — especially by purposefully investing in relationship with all those in our churches, neighborhoods, and communities.

♦ While we may not always be able to align ourselves with those in tension or those who seek reforms, we may be able to find some sort of broader teaming with them in the larger scheme of our Christian mission.

- Even if we judge someone's perspective to be errant or harmful, there is humility in acknowledging that their efforts may still bring about good we would not anticipate.

- When we're unsure of or threatened by the positions or motives of our detractors, one possible response is to surrender those concerns to God.

Chapter 10

Should I Stay
or Should I Go?

Unfortunately, committing to maintain relationships with others does not resolve every decision we face. It says little about the specific details themselves, about who we decide to formally align with, who we spend the most time with, where or if we go to church.

And I know there are many, both in the church and frustrated by it, who are worried I will conclude this book in a way that invalidates their positions — either in a way that dismisses the strength of tradition, the pillars of belief, or in a way that discards the valid concerns of those who are wounded by them.

Will I try to persuade readers to flee from their local churches? Or will I beg them to stay?

Neither option, of course, does my own experience justice. If I blindly were to tell you who are discouraged to plug back into your churches regardless of circumstances, I would be foolishly failing to value the relationship each person has with God by lifting my voice over whatever God might be stirring in you. Not to mention, I would be preserving my own hypocrisy in print for years to come because I would be giving out advice that I myself have not always been willing or able to follow.

Sadly, some church contexts can be genuinely stifling and unhealthy. At the very least, they can be repressing for people with certain types of gifts or dreams that may not be welcomed by their boards or congregations. And I also have to concede that God sometimes plants a vision in a person's heart that would best thrive somewhere other than the local church he or she is currently attending. Some visions might be better suited for a different style of church, a church in a larger or smaller city, or a church in a different region, for example. In acknowledging this, I do still suggest you use *extreme* caution and exercise fierce patience when exiting your local congregation.

Don't hear me wrong. I don't think God intended for there to be locks on the church doors and bars on the church windows. But I do think we have a duty to end well, to ensure that our motives and attitudes align with what we know of God, and to resist fleeing out of frustration, impatience, or refusal to grow beyond our own weaknesses. I have concluded, instead, that sometimes it may be best, and even God-directed, to stay in the local church, while at other times it may be best, and even God-directed, to leave. Depending on the situation, either choice could be appropriate.

THINGS TO DO IF YOU THINK
YOU'RE GOING TO LEAVE

The choice to leave a church involves *discernment*, a word that in the wide spectrum of churchgoers is defined innumerable ways.

And so it is wise to use our reason, to pay attention to our gut instincts, to seek the feedback of other trusted voices, and to seek the wisdom of Christian tradition. And if ever there has been a time to shore up wisdom, it's now, in matters that stand to add to or detract from the unity of the church or to combine or divide the resources of those who follow after God.

One quick heart check to start with is this: When you pray about your situation, do you feel unresolved anger toward certain people in your local church; do you take pride knowing that bailing would prove something to someone? Do you suspect leaving the church would be running away from a problem instead of facing it?

I'm no prophet, but I do know the difference between a good feeling and a terrible feeling. I know the difference between feeling free and lighthearted and feeling plagued with sleepless, guilty nights. I'm a firm believer that if we go, we must do everything in our power to go in peace, in a spirit of blessing. And if we can't, if our stomachs are contorted into giant square knots, this is a red flag that we have more emotional and soul-level work to do. We still may end up choosing to leave in the end, but if we do so, we determine to do so at a later date with cleaner hearts and clearer thinking.

A second method of discernment is to check your motives and actions against God's Word. It's very unlikely that God would ask you to do something that goes against the ideal of right relationship upheld across the message of the Bible. If in leaving your local congregation you would commit some sort of scriptural infraction, like acting in pride or causing your brothers and sisters to stumble, you need to make a slower, more reasoned assessment of your situation.

But should you feel resolved in peace, good-hearted toward those you've shared communion with in the past, yet still conclude leaving a church is the best option, another wise safeguard beyond your own conscience is the voice of community.

Mentors are valuable, but I would like to add one caveat. When seeking the wisdom of community, it may be tempting to seek the ideas and perspective of only one group of people — the people who are likely to agree with the way you see things.

I would humbly offer what may be an unpopular or hard-to-hear suggestion: that you seek feedback from the following:

1. *People who have observed you in your daily life for a long period of time* — in other words, those who may have insight into your patterns of behavior and your tendencies in dealing with conflict, and who possibly also know the other parties involved. Others — relatives who live in a different region, friends you run into at conferences, leaders within your tribe who live across the globe, or online friends you've connected with for years — will likely contribute valuable ideas as well but act in your own best interest by heavily weighting the voice of those who share your everyday habitat.

2. *People who have guts.* Talk to the people who have previously demonstrated they have the conviction and fortitude to stand up to you when they disagree. Yes, in the temporary scheme of things, it's more fun and affirming to go to your biggest cheerleaders and most committed yes-men and yes-women. But if your goal is to find health for yourself, to move toward long-term well-being for yourself and your church, you'd be wise to speak purposefully with those who will be honest about their perceptions.

3. *People who bring different kinds of life experience and tradition to the table.* For instance, as I wrote the first edition of this

book, I was particularly aware of the need to hear the advice of diverse groups within the larger Christian community. Hence, I talked to my Southern Baptist church-planting father, my emergent nondenominational church staffers, my contemplative pastor friend, a former foreign missionary, my Free Methodist college chaplain, my university's Quaker vice president and president, my mystic-loving mentor, my former speech professor — and the list goes on. While seeking their input, I not only got to hear a wide sampling of perspectives, but because most of them are older than me, I also got to tune in to an especially precious voice: the voice of experience.

Sometimes I think that nothing better illustrates the beauty of Christ's intergenerational following than the wisdom discovered when a young person's ideas about the church collide with the ideas of his or her parents' or grandparents' generation. The church of yesterday won't let us rush too far ahead, but the church of tomorrow won't let us stay where we are. We constantly have to examine opposing perspectives and find a way to cooperatively evolve, to improve our character, and to bolster our weaknesses to help balance the church of the future.

If, after consulting with this wide sampling of the larger Christian community, the consensus is something like, "I really respect the way you've handled yourself with this church thing, and I think it is clear that God is directing you to a new place," then it's a good sign you're on solid ground. If you hear this from your pastor or other leaders in your current church, this is a particularly good sign. You are free to move on with the wind of support at your back.

However, if the consistent response of your community is to point to ugly attitudes at work in your heart, to express concern over damaged relationships, or to draw attention to issues you could still better resolve, you would be acting in your own best interest to listen well. Rather than become angry and defensive, which is an understandable and perhaps instinctive response, you may set yourself up for the best outcome when you determine to treat these people like your personal trainers. The path they've laid out for you may be difficult; they may ask you to overcome obstacles, to succeed at things you've never succeeded at before, but you can choose to trust that the pain and hard work will make you stronger and healthier. Months or years from now, you may look back and find that the voices of others saved you from rash decision making and helped you to find peace, to better resolve frustrations, and to set a pace that promoted your own well-being.

And don't worry. If the community around you hesitates to applaud your proposed exit, it doesn't mean your ideas are not valid or you won't eventually employ them in a different context. It just means that today may not be the day that provides your ideas the best launch and the optimal chance of success.

Lastly, after listening closely to the larger Christian community, I suggest you might be able to pick up a thing or two from studying Christian tradition. You wouldn't believe some of the things the church has fought over and held councils over and killed people over! Reading old history books can help put your current dilemma into better focus. Somehow, realizing that people were tied to stakes and lit on fire for believing in a personal relationship with God makes your church's failure to visit the hospital when you broke your leg seem less of an offense.

When you honor these safeguards of checking your spirit, receiving the feedback of community, and seeking the perspective of the past, you give yourself the gift of clearer sight in answering the questions that lie ahead.

DISCUSSION QUESTIONS

1. Have you ever contemplated leaving your church? Or have you left a church in the past? What kinds of things tempted you to leave, and what kinds of things tempted you to stay?

2. Do you, like the author, believe that staying or leaving could be the right decision, depending on the circumstances? Why or why not?

3. What do you think of the author's suggestion that the disillusioned pay attention to their gut instincts, seek feedback, and seek the wisdom of Christian tradition? Why do you think the author suggested filtering the decision through all three of these actions rather than, say, just considering one's own gut instincts?

4. Is there any advice you would add for people who are torn between staying with their church and leaving it?

5. Have you ever considered leaving church but ended up staying? Explain how that worked out for you.

KEY IDEAS

◆ A good-hearted person can be torn between wanting to leave a church to explore alternative ways of doing things and wanting to stay in the church out of loyalty to his or her current community.

◆ It can be helpful to pray and seek the Holy Spirit and to tune in to our gut instincts as we do so. If we feel free and lighthearted to move on, that would be a good sign. If we lose sleep and feel weighed down by guilt, it should give us pause.

◆ Seeking the advice of people who have observed our daily patterns over time, people who have demonstrated they have the courage to tell us the truth, and people who have different life experiences that might yield different perspectives can be helpful.

◆ We also might gain perspective by reading a bit about the sometimes life-threatening struggles that have been part of the church's history. This may help us sort out whether our own frustrations might be exaggerated in comparison to those who faced persecution for their disagreement.

Chapter 11

Church at Home, Church on the Road

I first considered the option of deepening my investment in the church, rather than withdrawing it, almost by accident. During a conversation with my pastor, I told him that after college I intended to shift my efforts away from the church to the nonprofit sector (which to me seemed more focused on engaging *all* people).

His response? "Sarah, I hear your dissatisfaction, but no matter what your grievance is, the church remains *the* institution that Christ himself appointed to carry his hope to the world."

My pastor was a very smart man. However, despite the validity of his reminder, my idealism was not easily distracted. "Well then," I countered, "show me the church that will engage these people, and I will show you the church where I'll invest my life." I said it almost facetiously, as a tongue-in-cheek challenge to a friend, but the idea stuck in my mind.

Several years and many hard conversations later, the pastor

hired me to be the director of Reach — the first official outreach-oriented arm of our church.

Then an alternative to leaving dawned. *Huh. This is another option.* If my local church was willing, I realized, perhaps I could help lead the charge in recovering some of the values I felt were underrepresented in our congregation. By giving me the chance to take ownership in its direction, this local church helped prevent me from walking away from the church at large. It made me a true partner in its mission. And it allowed me time to understand the value of Christian community well enough that I would never want to live without it.

I can't help but wonder if that's what many experiencing disillusionment need most: local churches that will allow us to take ownership in where the global church is going, churches that will let us be true partners in determining how to carry out Christ's mission to our world.

STAYING WHERE YOU ARE

Here are a few tips I've picked up, mostly through my own mistakes, for those considering staying:

Be honest about your feelings from the start. Let people help you find solutions that will make you stay. By quietly brooding over your concerns, you may plant seeds of pent-up anger or frustration that will eventually surface in ways that won't help your cause. Get to the point as early as you can and focus not on the problem but on the solution. A good way to engage the discussion might be, "I have really enjoyed my experience at this church. I've been thinking about this particular area of ministry, and I think it would be a good fit here because it is a little bit different than some of our other ministries."

Don't talk as if you have all the answers. This is an unadmirable tendency among some Christian groups of which I confess I have been part. We like to read the latest books or hear the latest speakers and think to ourselves, *This person has discovered* the *way God intended for his church to function.* We turn people's ideas into crazes that everybody who is anybody must implement to be at the forefront of the next wave of history. Maybe this is because it is just easier to declare we have found *the* answer than to go on day after day only gradually growing toward greater understanding.

Resolve to take whatever opportunities God presents you, regardless of size. If your dream opportunity doesn't present itself, take whatever opportunities do arise. Before I ever was given my outreach post at my church, for example, I led an outreach-oriented small group and led a volunteer relief trip while overseeing the church's children's and youth ministries. Both of these were ways of being faithful to what God was doing in my spirit as I waited, albeit impatiently, for bigger opportunities. Likewise, when I left my staff position at this church, I continued to try to take small opportunities to be active in the global outreach arena. Because I was no longer employed by a church, I decided one small thing I could do was begin to post articles on the web that could assist churches in doing the kinds of things I was passionate about. In the process, I stumbled onto an opportunity to share my ideas on a larger scale through publishing the first edition of this book.

Don't rush it. Maybe God is showing you a small glimpse of a bigger opportunity he will bring into play down the road. If things aren't moving ahead as fast as you wish, take time to prepare yourself for what you think God wants to do through you in the future. Get a degree or additional training; learn to articulate the importance of your ministry idea using solid, biblical evidence; fine-tune your organizational skills. There is a lot you can do to get yourself ready for what's next.

In encouraging people to reengage our local congregations, I'd like to leave church leaders with the same challenge I voiced to my friend and pastor: Show us the church that will engage our concerns, and we will show you the church where coming generations will invest their lives.

STAYING THEN GOING

There's another option that exists somewhere between staying and going, and that's staying long enough to prepare yourself to transition to a new thing when the timing is right.

From my observations, a good way to start a new community — whether it be small-group oriented, neighborhood based, nonprofit centered, or whatever else you can think of — is to invite a group of similarly impassioned, somewhat like-minded people to pray and study God's ideals together.

This is how my dad's previous two churches got started. While he was a pastor at one church, God gave him the opportunity to get involved in a home Bible study elsewhere in the region. The Bible study was just that — a Bible study. There was no stated invitation to join a church or to spearhead any new, permanent Christian community. The people who attended just hung out together and jointly explored what God was doing in their lives. Left in God's hands, it wasn't long before some of the ideas gained incredible momentum and a church was born.

Now, if you drive down Lewis Avenue in Ida, Michigan, you will see a local church where a cornfield used to be. And soon, if you drive down Ida West in Petersburg, Michigan, you will find a church where an adjoining lot to a factory used to be.

To this day, whenever I stand in the building that my dad's church attendees helped to build, whenever I walk around the property we prayed over long before the Department of Natural Resources ever said the land was buildable, a powerful realization consumes me. Because my dad and a group of like-minded people pursued what God was doing in their spirits, one more branch of God's global church, representing Christ's ideals to our world, took root. There was one more place that unashamedly marked itself as the home of Christian community — where people might see the spiritual and earthly worlds merge. Where people could come in contact with Jesus. Because of my dad's and others' faith, Ida and Petersburg have a little less corn and fewer weedy lots but hopefully a lot more Jesus.

Along these lines, I offer you some of my own learnings about moving on:

Don't pressure yourself to stay for the wrong reasons. While I have been careful to discourage people from leaving a church for the wrong reason, I also have to acknowledge that it can be easy to stay at your local church for the wrong reasons. You may be tempted to stay because of familiarity, nostalgia, or even to prove a point. But all of these reasons will result in less satisfaction, less blessing, and less gain for the kingdom than doing what God wants you to do.

If you are seeking familiarity and comfort, let me remind you that you will never be safer than when you are pursuing what God desires. If you grieve the loss of your former memories, let me assure you that your memories will grow even sweeter when you realize how they have prepared you for God's new tasks in your life. And, lastly, though I don't think we should strive to prove a point to anyone in our former congregations, you can take heart knowing, as did the disciples who stood before Gamaliel, that when God is really moving in you, you will not have to prove it to anyone. People will notice.

Don't give your life to a movement other than the one embodied in the teachings and life of Jesus. There are all kinds of "good" causes in the world, but there is only one cause that trumps all the rest — and that is the cause of Christ. Don't get sucked into religious movements that seem to be fueled only by a desire to be different or cool. Learn from and appreciate movements that are driven by a desire to know Christ, to be like him, and to be faithful to his mission.

Similarly, if a movement seems to churn out disciples who are chronic complainers, if they produce leaders who live to bask in the spotlight, if they leave their converts without grounding or teaching, if they sacrifice their local congregations or families for their cause, then be suspicious. Converts to the church are not perfect. But if movements are grounded in God's aims, then their common bond should be that their disciples are morphing into people who look, smell, sound, and taste increasingly more like Jesus.

Be faithful to notice the signals God is prompting in you. Do you have some far-out-there vision? Does this idea keep reoccurring to you, no matter how you try to push it out of your mind? Over time, do you feel an increasing push to actually act on your idea? Do you even feel that by not moving on it you could possibly be disobeying God? Then tune in. This *might* be God.

Take time to nurture a support system. Having people with diverse gifts — teaching, administrative, and hospitality talents, for example — always bolsters the health of any group or organization. Though I don't think it's always necessary, it usually makes sense to wait to advertise your ministry until you actually have people to help lead your new initiative! If God blesses, and thirty or a hundred people join you right away, you'll likely want some support to be able to wisely steward the opportunity he has given you.

If no one arises to help you lead this initiative, you might want to consider whether it is really the right time to push ahead. If you still feel God is prompting you onward, consider gaining necessary support by finding a local church or organization to mentor you or, if that is not available, establishing a board of advisers that can assist you along the way.

Also, don't rule out coming alongside a person or group already doing something closely related to what you have in mind. Joining someone else further along in the journey gives you a chance to learn on the job and puts you in contact with networks of people who may be similarly impassioned. Time spent cooperating with an existing ministry might save you years of mistakes and setbacks if and when God gives you a leadership post in a similar venue in the future. And it might be a gift to exhausted leaders who have poured out their lives to finally have some reinforcements!

Be open to many different possible outcomes. If you start a small group to pursue your ideas and it becomes a *really* small group — even the world's smallest small group — and all you accomplish is growing a few people with similar passions, you still haven't wasted any time or effort.

After college, our best man, Wes, and a few of our friends moved into the south side of our city and engaged an idea they called The Plan. The Plan consisted of four people — Wes, Miguel, Tanya, and Nikki — who partnered with probably a dozen more people to build relationships with our city's diverse people groups while living in two side-by-side urban apartments. Over time, they hoped to move on and serve in some major urban area together.

Unfortunately, or maybe fortunately, depending on how you look at it, the foursome and their friends didn't end up staying together for the long run. But while their teaming didn't result in the four of them together serving God in *a* city, it did result in them serving God separately in four different cities. So God's purposes were served by their one-time grouping.

Live life large. If you still feel uncertain about stepping away from the comfortable, you might want to begin with some small-scale initiatives that fall in line with your bigger vision. Admit to God that you are scared of full-on pursuing your biggest ideas, but pledge allegiance to follow him if he is trying to prompt you in bigger directions. Ask that as you take a step forward, he will give you further clarity about whether to continue.

Once it becomes apparent God is doing something new in you, celebrate, but more than anything — go after it! Give it absolutely everything you've got. There is no better experience than letting God use your personal journey to do his work in others.

Expect the transition to be difficult. The grass may seem greener on the other side of your local congregation's fence, but a lot of times that is just the sun getting in your eyes. The biggest difference between attending someone else's church and starting your own version of Christian community is that you are now no longer the complainer but the one to whom people complain. Welcome to the world of your former church staff and denominational leaders.

Protect your health. A lesson I learned early on and have sadly had to relearn many times since, and which I have confidently repeated to everyone I know, is this: Christians should err on the side of health. Err on the side of doing too much to exercise your head, heart, and spirit. Err on the side of too much accountability, of holding yourself to a higher standard than necessary, of putting boundaries in place that may sometimes restrict you. Err on the side of hearing warnings that surface along the way. Err on the side of not participating in behaviors that diminish your capacity to live your vision. Guard your ability to persevere at all costs. You will never feel worse than the day you have to give up opportunities to participate in God's mission because your spiritual health has been compromised.

Don't tie happiness to one specific outcome. It's not important that you instantly create a Christian community in which all your major concerns are addressed. What *is* important is that you attempt to know God for all he is willing to reveal himself to be and that you attempt to respond to everything he shows you along the way. There's a chance that God will point you toward an outcome different than the one you were originally aiming for. Be willing to walk on an evolving path. If you insist on only pursuing your pet causes and concerns, you may end up disappointed one day to find your version of church shows the same flaws as the congregations and movements that once disillusioned you. Success is not being perfect, or even being *more* perfect than your previous churches. Success is being faithful to what God is doing in your life.

Maintain the mainline spiritual disciplines. In your rush to grab a spot on the nightly news as the most brilliant up-and-coming Christian community in your area, don't draw your new identity from forsaking your old one. Remember the practices — biblical teaching, discipleship, evangelism, prayer, worship — that made your former churches strong. Continue to draw from those, allowing yourself to bear up what you believe in instead of constantly positioning yourself by what you're opposing.

Formulate a plan for where and how you will continue to experience community if you leave your church. Map out resources that will help replace the benefits of Christian community you will lose in the process. How will you engage the Bible, express worship, experience life-on-life learning, live in accountability, draw inspiration, employ your spiritual gifts, and soak up leadership training? In other words, don't dive into the ocean without a boat. And don't launch out in a boat unless you know how to sail one.

Review what living in the tension between "what is" and "what should be" may have taught you. There is no sense in learning a hard lesson twice. Some uphill battles are worth the strain, thanks to the endurance and courage they build in you and in others as well. Remember the truths you have discovered during this journey; instant message them on the screens of your heart so that you will not lose them.

If at all possible, embark on your departure with a mutual exchange of blessings. When I left my staff position at my local church, I sat down and looked my pastor in the eyes and said, "For all the good and bad, I am not willing to leave here without giving you my blessing and receiving yours in return." Because of this intentional effort to stay teamed in our global cause even in my local resignation, this pastor remains a friend and valuable resource in my ongoing spiritual formation to this day.

I firmly believe that we best usher in our most ideal future when we make peace with and own the lessons of our past. And I lament the hardships that many encounter when they march forward without learning to bless those they have been teamed with in the past. This inability to find unity creates unfortunate chapters in the church's history.

Acknowledge that God might have something different in store for your local church than he has for you. The time may come when what God is stirring in you might be entirely different from the priorities your church identifies for itself. Rather than assume they've lost the beat of the Spirit's rhythm, I've learned to accept that God might be showing them something different than he is showing me. (That, as it turns out, is how God gets done more than one thing in the world at a time.) Besides, I am not responsible for what every other person does with his or her following of Jesus. I am just responsible for what I do with mine. If I determine that because of my own passions I cannot stand with a local church's specific agenda, I also resolve that I will not stand against them.

Don't drag anyone's name or ideas through the mud on your way out the door. Whew. This is a hard lesson to learn, but a valuable one. Odds are, most people in the congregation are not going to understand the intricate details of why your desires can't be accomplished in their local church. Giving them reason to criticize people or things that wouldn't normally be on their radar is a very sketchy decision. Doing so can decrease their ability to respect, receive from, and be grown by their local church. And whether your local church is hitting your groove or not, God is still working there, continuing what he started. You wouldn't want to take away from that, would you?

DISCUSSION QUESTIONS

1. The first half of this chapter contains tips to keep in mind if you decide to stay in a church and work through your disillusionment. Which of these tips seem most helpful to you?
2. The second half of this chapter contains ideas for using the remaining time with your congregation to prepare for the next steps you think you will take down the road. Which of these seem most helpful to you?

KEY IDEA

- ◆ Both staying at a local church or moving on could be an appropriate response to hardship, but in either case, we are wise to seek resolution, counsel, and peace wherever possible.

Chapter 12

Your Grandmother's Church

This isn't church as usual."

"We don't do the typical worship service here."

"This isn't your grandmother's church."

These are statements snagged from worship services I've attended or gleaned from the "About" pages of church websites from around the country.

They tout laid-back environments full of "real" people, "people like you," people in "jeans and T-shirts." No hymns. No pews. Come as you are.

These descriptors are inviting and comfortable. They do what they're designed to do — communicate a local church's commitment to being involved in culture, to being pertinent and savvy, to using creative means to "do life together."

It is only fair to note that these statements are often attached to sincerely loving, brilliant churches marked by noticeable vitality and a lot of people much like myself in many ways. But as someone who has traveled to and participated in conferences and church gatherings around the country, and as someone who has at times championed a "not usual" church, I want to let you in on a little secret: *There are so many churches who describe themselves as "not church as usual" that the next generation is going to have to say, "This is church as usual," to set themselves apart.*

What we mean when we offer these kinds of statements, I think, is we want you to feel welcome, we want you to know this church is not dead and empty and dusty. That here, there is a fresh, vibrant community worth engaging and you're going to learn and experience things worth your time.

All good and well. But the language we use to express these intentions oftentimes is anti-language. Instead of saying who we are, we communicate our own identity by announcing who we are not — as if we believe the faith and religion that got messy in the hands of those before us will stay unblemished in ours. As if we will be what they are not, fix what they have broken, succeed where they failed.

The older I get, the more I hesitate to use or buy into language like this. Instead, I hypothesize that part of what we're learning in the ongoing discussions about disillusionment is that our disillusionment is more the result of our own choices — our expectations, the way we bestow admiration, yes, maybe even sometimes our sense of entitlement — than it is about some party outside of us.

What we're dealing with, as it turns out, is much bigger than the need for accountability for church leaders or the need for new church models. This monster is soooo much bigger than that.

The let-down expectations, abuse of power, negligence? Those aren't issues that surface only in churches or Christian spheres. They surface in institutions of all kinds, in families, in schools, in companies, in nonprofit organizations, in law enforcement, in the judicial system, in militaries, in governments. And they show neither mercy nor favor. These disappointments rain down on the just and unjust alike, showing no more shyness in arriving in this generation than the last, no more reservations in showing up in this country than the others. When we experience disillusionment, what we are really staring in the face is the timeless, boundaryless problem of human suffering.

And if that is truly the case, if frustrations are ours as a human race to own, if they will be an ever-present reality in every generation, then suddenly a good source of wisdom and hope might be to find someone who has been around for generations — maybe a couple thousand years — and find out what they have learned, what they have to say about the ongoing human search for meaning, purpose, and truth.

And that is when some of us might find ourselves back at a familiar set of doors, taking in an old iron bell, a steeple, some stained glass. That old familiar church.

Perhaps, then, the truly poignant, the truly triumphant cry is not "We are not our grandmother's church." Perhaps the most profound and penetrating truth is ... that we are.

Or as Jonathan Martin, pastor of a Charlotte, North Carolina, church called Renovatus, perhaps said best:

> We ARE your grandmother's church. And your great-grandmother's church. And your great-great-grandmother's church! The desire to cut ourselves off from those who came before us is no virtue. The sense of rootlessness and individuality of our culture — the ruthless attempt of social and technological forces to convince us that we can

be story-less people who are making it up as we go, is a posture not for the gospel to adapt to but to oppose. We are forever tethered to our grandmother's church, and this is as it should be. Our grandmother's church has given us many good gifts.[13]

This seems consistent with one of my favorite chapters in the Bible, John 17, where Jesus prayed for his disciples — not just his current disciples, but for all those who would trek after him in years to come. For your great-great-great-grandmothers, for your great-grandmothers, for your grandmothers, for you, and for all those who will come after you.

> "My prayer is not for them alone. I pray also for those who will believe in me through their message, that all of them may be one, Father, just as you are in me and I am in you. May they also be in us so that the world may believe that you have sent me. I have given them the glory that you gave me, that they may be one as we are one — I in them and you in me — so that they may be brought to complete unity. Then the world will know that you sent me and have loved them even as you have loved me." (vv. 20 – 23)

It is with this cry for unity with the timeless church of Christ, then, that we perhaps realize the true meaning of the statement this book began with: "We are not alone." Instead, we stand side by side with all of humankind, before us and after us, including our Savior, who took on flesh and bones to join our race. And we stand, like all those who've gone before us, and we face the flaws and dysfunctions of this planet that rear their heads both inside and outside the church's walls.

With this awareness, perhaps we come to better understand why the Bible names the church as the bride of Christ — because the church is not just the glowing being we encountered on some enchanted day and with whom we stumbled head over heels into love at first sight. She is also at times the worn-down lover, too tired to get out of bed, too sick to brush her teeth, too cranky to say or do the right thing. But the longer we are with her and the more we observe this paradoxical mix of poise and flaws, grace and clumsiness, glory and grit, the more we somehow love her. And this act of rising and stretching to love an imperfect being as imperfect beings holds deep, enduring beauty.

"Any idiot can find God in the sunset," Lillian Daniel, author of *When Spiritual but Not Religious Is Not Enough*, says. "What is remarkable is finding God in the context of flawed, human community and a tradition bigger than you are with people who may not reflect God back to you in your own image."[14] So, to my disillusioned friends, I say this: If we work hard to maintain our relationship with the generations before us, I hope and believe our older, healthier counterparts will faithfully put an arm around us and support us through this shadowy season. This is not always easy, as they sometimes have to absorb the brunt of our emotions and they sometimes have to mourn the loss of some of their traditions in order to guide us into our newly shared future.

My hope for those veteran members of the faith is that they will not panic that the church of this generation won't be a carbon copy of the church of the previous generation; that they will realize we don't have their exact background or skill sets and that we don't see the world from their perspective; and that this makes sense because the methods that won awards in their generation may not be the most effective methods for reaching ours.

I hope they will read the most recent statistics about church attendance and spirituality and see more than just cold, clinical studies. I pray they will look past the unoccupied rows at church and notice the vital signs that often only become evident by listening with a stethoscope to a sometimes disenchanted, disappointed culture. I pray they will realize the church of our generation *is* breathing, that our heart is beating, and that we need their help to complete our rite of passage in carrying the church toward tomorrow.

I beg of our seniors, and of those in better health than us, to come alongside us and help us see when we're operating too much in the gray zones, help us draw those important boundaries, help us understand the value of tradition, encourage us to develop the characteristics we lack so that we can take our identity as the church seriously.

While clinging to the wisdom of veteran believers, I come to the final option for responding to disillusionment with the church.

What if after all of this you still can't move forward?

Then don't. Don't make any hasty decisions. Not today anyway.

If you can't run toward the church, then walk. If you can't walk, then stand and stare in its direction. If you can't stand, then sit on the ground. If you are too exhausted to sit, then lie down. But keep your hand outstretched and open to the possibility of engaging it somewhere down the road.

Take a break. And as you escape into retreat, please, for your own well-being, be careful what you say and be cautious about the messages you surround yourself with — especially if something particularly tragic happened in your own church experience. It might be wise to acknowledge that not everyone's experience with church has been equally harmful, that there might be more positive experiences in store beyond this, and that you may not be serving your own best interests or the interests of others by widely circulating every jaded thought that comes into your head.

Instead, be honest. There's nothing wrong with saying, "I realize God wanted us to be a part of Christian community, but right now I am just too hurt and too frustrated to be able to function healthily in that setting. I need some time to evaluate what I believe about organized religion. In the meantime, I would love to hang out with you. I don't have it all figured out yet, but I am not giving up on God or his desires for his followers yet." Not only does this kind of confession promote understanding, but it may help you build a support system. Perhaps the people who come around you in such moments will listen well and be your church in the moments when you choose not to attend a church building.

This wounded, flawed church taking care of its wounded, flawed members (and ex-members), in suits or jeans, with hymns or not, as usual or not as usual, grandmothers or grandbabies, is the raw, substance-filled, movie-worthy romance that lets me return to feelings of love for the church again.

DISCUSSION QUESTIONS

1. Does your church or another church you know make a point to welcome others by talking about what a casual, "come as you are" environment it provides? Have you ever heard anyone make a statement like "This isn't your grandmother's

church"? What are the positive ideas being communicated by these statements? How might these statements limit people's understanding of church?

2. Do you find yourself relating more to the perspective of the disillusioned? If so, do you find it easy to seek out veteran members of the faith as mentors? What, if anything, prevents you from doing so more often?

3. Do you find yourself relating more to the perspective of the veteran leader? If so, do you find it easy to offer guidance to those younger than yourself? What, if anything, prevents you from doing so more often?

KEY IDEA

◆ Perhaps it isn't the newest ideas that should be touted the loudest. After all, they haven't been tested long enough to see if they will even survive. Perhaps the best ideas, to the contrary, are the ones that have already stood the test of time, the ones championed by believers long before us.

Chapter 13

No One Owes You an Explanation

One day, in a moment of dark reflection, a friend asked me, "Why do you feel like you need someone to give you an explanation for your disappointments?"

I staggered backward.

Why *did* I need an explanation? Why *was* I letting my own peace depend on other people's willingness to express regret for the pain I had experienced?

As I tried to answer this question, other questions arose. Wasn't I — a member of the global church, not to mention a former staff member in a local church setting — just as responsible as any other party for how the church failed its members? Why didn't *I* ever feel the need to apologize on behalf of the church to those who had been hurt?

When I thought about it, I realized that most people never get an apology for the way the church hurts them. Sure, we all do our part in contributing to the church's shared mistakes, but when it comes time to take the blame, we seem to lose our individuality. All of a sudden, the church is just one faceless, nameless, ownerless institution that can't own up to its failures.

I decided this was not okay. It wasn't okay for me or for others fighting off disillusionment to experience pain at the hand of the church and then have the church just keep on plodding forward as if nothing had ever happened. Somewhere along the line, I thought, someone should legitimize and apologize for the wounds of the injured.

I wondered how the church could help release people from this type of pain — the kind of confusing pain you feel when it seems as though God himself, through his church, has rejected or insulted you. I wondered whether any one of us could help dissolve some of the burdens church people carry by looking them square in the eye and admitting that the church has not always been what it was supposed to be.

The more I thought about the idea, the more real it became to me. I found myself wanting to help resolve the sorrow attached to so many people's interactions with the church. I wanted to tell as many people as I could, face-to-face, "This pain and rejection is not what God intended for you to experience in Christian community. Please forgive us for the times when we have failed to act like the community of Jesus followers we claim to be."

As "out there" as this idea seemed at one level, I had a strong motivation to see it executed. So I decided to put forth a strange request. I asked the elders of my local church — ironically, a church I had tried to leave and returned to more than once — if I could offer an apology. I told them I wanted to ask forgiveness not only for the hurt I may have inflicted on others but for the hurt people may have experienced at the hand of the church at large. Because of a very unique set of circumstances, this church, which happened to be undergoing some reevaluation, found the spirit of the idea appropriate for an upcoming meeting.

I soon found myself sitting on the stage and saying, "Some of you are long overdue for an apology." I proceeded then to cry through a lengthy series of apologies, intertwined with jokes about how mascara (which now was running down my face) was the world's worst invention.

When I finished, my reception was overwhelming. Dozens of people made the effort to find me before they left that evening. Grabbing me by the sleeve, they told me, "Thank you *soooo* much. That was so important for me to hear. You have no idea how that released me from some of the pain and bitterness I had been experiencing."

Honestly, by that point, I barely cared about their benefits. I was experiencing the climax of my own freedom from burden and bitterness — quite possibly the freest moment in my entire Christian experience. In that moment, I didn't feel disillusionment's sting anymore.

I emerged from that night thinking that even just a few minutes of experiencing such intense, shared grace was so sweet that I would not want to live my life without it again. And I resolved that in the future I would be better at noticing opportunities to offer apologies and to usher in what little piece of God's grace I might give to others.

I can't help thinking that this might be one of those times. A chance to acknowledge the hurt swirling around beneath the surface of the larger Christian community. And a chance to express my regret that the church at large has sometimes hurt people on a historical and international scale. And so, people of our world,

I want to offer an apology to you on behalf of those who try, and sometimes fail, to represent God to our world.

To lead pastors and missionaries and leaders of movements, I'm sorry for the times when our spotlight has left you sunburned. We've often encouraged you to perform as though you are always onstage, waiting for the affirmation of our applause. But there are times when you too should be allowed to be privately human, to make mistakes or experience grief that people don't print in the bulletin or pass through the prayer chain. I am profoundly sorry for the times we have squeezed you under the world's most powerful microscope and tediously examined all your flaws.

Pastors, I'm sorry for the times we have made you the church referee, forced to make split-second decisions, knowing that no matter what you chose, half the gym would criticize the call. I'm sorry that you have lost sleep and tears and maybe a little blood, bearing the weight of heavy decisions. I'm sorry that we've sometimes squashed you between a rock and a hard place, and when you finally chiseled your way out, we criticized your methodology. Our 20/20 hindsight makes the "right" call seem so ridiculously simple that we've often been outraged that you missed it.

I'm sorry our behaviors might have forced you into some unhealthy habits that took a toll on your own emotional well-being and that of your family. I know that sometimes you had to develop calluses — thick skin that could sustain you through the times when no one seemed to support you. And I'm sorry that those calluses sometimes spread to your heart, so that you couldn't connect with your congregation any longer. I'm sorry we may have forced you to be hardheaded, to charge ahead in warrior-style leadership because it seemed impossible to get a consensus from your perpetually divided people.

And perhaps more than anything, I regret the times when we have affirmed you in ways that put you in the place of our Savior, the times we have been carelessly willing to follow you in any direction and put our hopes and faith in your intelligence or leadership above even the God you serve.

I'm sorry this misplaced allegiance to you, rather than Christ, may have brought out the worst in you. That it may have launched an addiction in some of you, encouraging you to chase after the admiration of others before the blessing of God. I'm sorry for a wide range of destructive behaviors this may have caused: perfectionism, depression, willingness to exploit others, fear of failure, oversensitivity, guilt, restlessness. I'm sorry that we sometimes tied accountability to whether the church was bigger or flashier instead of whether it was deeper or holier.

I am so sorry, pastors, that you can do a million things right and still be nailed to the wall for the one thing you do wrong. And I'm sorry too few people have had the guts to voice their concerns to your face rather than to their small groups. I am especially sorry for the guilt and rejection that you may have been unable to separate yourself from when people criticized your local church or the church at large. You have taken responsibility on more than one occasion for problems to which you never contributed.

I read the following quote from Teddy Roosevelt, and it reminds me of my admiration for you pastors who continue year after year:

> It is not the critic who counts, not the man who points out how the strong man stumbled, or where the doer of deeds could have done them better. The credit belongs to the man who is actually in the arena; whose face is marred by

dust and sweat and blood; who strives valiantly; who errs and comes up short again and again; who knows the great enthusiasms, the great devotions, and spends himself in a worthy cause; who, at best, knows in the end the triumph of high achievement; and who, at the worst, if he fails, at least fails while daring greatly, so that his place shall never be with those cold and timid souls who know neither victory nor defeat.[15]

Lastly, I'm sorry for the loss you experienced when friends and team members walked away from your shared mission. Despite your obligation to bless their departures, it couldn't have been easy to watch these companions exit the journey. I'm sorry for the disappointments you felt in your soul when yet another person discarded the church context that you could not as easily abandon. Thank you so much for staying the course.

To the families of pastors and missionaries, whose identities within their local church families is often so tightly tied to their spouses' or parents' posts, I humbly apologize. I'm sorry for the times when your individuality got swallowed up by titles like "missionary kid" or "pastor's wife." I'm sorry for the times when this loss of personhood stripped you of your own right to grow and think and forge new ministries of your own. I'm sorry people saw you for whose son you are or whose wife you are rather than for who *you* are.

I'm sorry you sometimes gave up your husband or father or mother to lead the "world" into wholeness, but no one seemed to notice when you or your family were hurting. I'm sorry we sometimes thought Christmas cookies and greeting cards could sustain you through all twelve months of the year. I'm sorry we failed to realize that your family is human as well, that you experience pain and hurt in the everyday and therefore have a much more consistent need for encouragement and gratitude. I'm sorry if we fostered an environment that didn't allow you to talk about when you were hurting or in trouble.

I'm sorry for the unrealistic expectations we sometimes anchored to your lifestyles. That we thought you should somehow be able to grow up or grow old without making the mistakes so many of the rest of us are permitted to make. That we pressured you to be the example when sometimes you were the one who needed the extra support and maybe — just once or twice — we could have strived to be a role model for you.

Kids, I'm sorry for the times we have attacked your parents, not realizing you *were* old enough to know exactly what was going on. Not understanding that you felt each blow we delivered to your dad or mom. Not comprehending how we stripped the church of its warmth for you, how our actions made God's institution look like a monster who was thirsty for your parents' blood. I'm sorry our own carelessness, immaturity, or desire to be right took away the comfort and familiarity that had once made the local church feel like your second home.

Most of all, I'm sorry, kids, for the times you saw the local church deliver so much destruction that you lost your desire to be part of the church at all. I'm sorry for the times your gifts got short-circuited, for the moments when you went from wanting to be on a church staff yourself to wanting to avoid the church at all costs. And on that note, I pray that you won't let our failures prevent you from exercising all the ideas and talent God put inside you. God's inspiration in your life is not what fell short. It was us. Go and grow up and, with our heartfelt blessing, lead the best local churches this world has ever seen. We believe in you.

To the elders of local churches, I'm sorry you have borne the criticism of people like me — who have never had to face the decisions you face or bear the responsibility you bear. I'm sorry for the long hours and late-night calls that enlarged your personal burden with churchwide issues of both enormous magnitude and minute detail. I'm sorry that in your faithfulness you have had to be the remnant crew who manned the church even when it seemed like a ship that would surely go down in the storm, and that you often did it without people caring how much responsibility you shouldered — or even knowing who the elders were, that is, until you made a decision they didn't like.

Please surrender your feelings of hurt, blame, and inadequacy and know that even in the times when you failed, you failed while attempting the noblest of causes. And let us give you, at least momentarily, our honor. Regardless of the outcome, rest easy knowing that whenever you tried to serve us through pure motives, you served us well. We are truly indebted to you, elders. And if we were smarter, we would thank you so much more often.

To church staff, I'm sorry there is no time clock to dispel the misconception you work only one day a week. I wish everyone in the church could log on to a website and see live-camera footage of you working ridiculous amounts of overtime, filling in when others bailed or coming early to open up and staying late to close. I sometimes wish your phone records were accessible to the public so people could readily see how many hours you spend counseling and troubleshooting to enhance their discipleship.

I'm sorry for the times when people became angry at you because you couldn't stretch yourself far enough, couldn't meet their every demand, couldn't be available every time they needed a resource or a word of encouragement. I'm sorry you were our "fix-it people," the ones we went to when *we* needed something, and that it all too rarely crossed our minds that you might have needed something along the way as well. I'm sorry you have had to live in a state of confusion — wondering at times whether you accomplished more good than you did bad. You did, by the way. Really. You'll never understand how much good you did.

I'm sorry for the times our commitment to you has failed to rival our commitment to our kids' bake sales or our home redecoration. That we have casually strolled by, noticed a problem we could help address, but then speed-walked in the other direction. I'm sorry for the times we have made you beg, go to vision-casting seminars, and read leadership books to manipulate us into doing what we should have been doing out of the natural motivation of our heart: helping serve our community. I'm sorry we sometimes looked for the least we could do instead of the most we could do. I'm sorry we called the church "*our* church" but that when it came to hard work, we sometimes translated this to mean "your" work.

I'm sorry we never realized that when we called at the last minute to say we couldn't fulfill our ministry obligation, we were only one of several backing out ten minutes prior to service start. I'm sorry that, as a result, you may have spent the first half hour or maybe the entire service running around panicked, trying to do multiple jobs at once to make sure our church's adults, teenagers, and children were served. I'm sorry that because of our failure to follow through on our commitments, you sometimes never got to sit down and go to church yourself, or that when you did, it was far less enjoyable because you constantly had to be concerned about how some area was short-staffed.

I'm sorry if our consumeristic expectations challenged you to become more efficient and more successful workaholics. I'm sorry if we made your job description so many miles long or piled so many hats onto your head that you were forced to live in a state of constant frustration, knowing that you could do nothing with excellence. I'm sorry for the times when we acted as if we were the only people you needed to please when, in reality, implementing our personal suggestions meant earning the disfavor of some other group in the church that held the opposite opinion. I'm sorry we sometimes backed you into a corner and then ridiculed you for sitting there.

I'm sorry we almost always forgot to send you that note of encouragement or to call and praise you for a job well done. And I'm even sorrier that we remembered somehow to call and let you have it when things didn't go the way we wanted.

To all of you who serve in this capacity, I pray God's fullness upon your lives. Though many times we Christians casually offer the promise "I'll pray for you," when it comes to you, I sincerely mean it. May God bless you and your families for your day-to-day faithfulness.

To volunteer leaders, I'm sorry for the times you came to the staff looking for clarity or support but walked away empty-handed. For the times the church staff have not been able to rise above their own challenges to source you, love you, invest in you, and maintain intimacy with you as they intended.

I'm sorry for the times when we church staff have acted as though you should have no life outside of our ministry areas, that you should be available any day of the week and any time of day to assist with routine and emergency operations. I'm sorry for the times we staffers became overdependent on those of you who could be counted on to do what you said you would do, how we pushed you to serve in too many services for too many months in a row without giving you an often needed reprieve.

I'm sorry for the times the staff expected you to put the rest of your life on hold but then failed to repay you by taking your suggestions and advice seriously. I am deeply sorry if we treated you as if you or your ideas didn't matter when you were — in many ways — the very backbone of our institution.

I'm sorry if we taught you to draw affirmation and motivation from the wrong place. If we spent more time training you to expand our attendance or increase our recognition than we spent encouraging you to truly, truly know God.

Let me just say what you have perhaps not heard often enough from the pulpit. And that is this: God cares far more — and I mean *far* more — about the condition of our souls and the genuineness of our relationship with him than he will ever care about our ability to keep all our services and ministries spinning flawlessly.

So if we have made you feel like you had to earn our favor, let me now encourage you to take the time to breathe deeply and really get to know our Jesus intimately. That is what is really important. Despite all our other encouragements, if you know one thing, know this: the moments when your heart is well ordered before our God are the moments when we are proudest of you.

To church attendees, I'm sorry for the weekends when you were overlooked. When no one said hi or remembered your name, when no one invited you to their small group or included you in their postservice plans. I'm sorry for the times when no one noticed you were absent or hurting — or both.

I'm sorry for the times when we offered you more programs than friendship, more books than honest dialogue, more encouragement to be like us than to be like God. I'm sorry for the times we asked you to serve in our ministries, to fill open service slots, without offering you the dignity of true friendship with us and our teams.

I'm sorry for the times we sent messages that would conflict with the example of Christ when he walked this earth. For the times we looked down our noses, scowled, or flashed cold stares in your direction. For the times we acted like we "on the inside" were somehow better than you "on the outside" and made you feel as if, by struggling uphill, you might someday be "good enough" to make it into our inner circles — to be one of "us."

I'm sorry for the times we pushed you too hard and asked you to take steps that you were not ready to take, to carry burdens you were not ready to bear. And, on the other hand, I'm sorry for the times we let you keep our seats warm but never prodded you to shed your anonymity and join in the game. I'm sorry for the times we tried to be your heroes, to hide our flaws from you instead of just letting you help us and love us and understand us for who we are.

I am endlessly sorry for the times when our failures have misrepresented God, made you doubt the Bible, or jaded you toward the church at large. Please know that it was us, and not Jesus, who failed you. And if you never set your foot in a church again, please know it is God who hears you in the stillness and distance of where you are and who will trump our narrow minds in welcoming you into the kingdom if you align yourself with him.

Forgive us for the times we failed to be the Christian community God wanted you to experience. You deserved better.

To those outside the church, I'm sorry for the times we underassessed your intelligence by assuming a few "cool" service elements, rather than real relationships, would draw you into our churches.

I'm sorry for the times we presented Christianity as a three-step plan to be read and signed as if it were some type of credit application. That we sometimes acted as though Christianity and Christ were so simple and tidy that we could neatly package them inside a little box that you should be able to open and transplant into your spirit without any questions or hesitation. I'm sorry we sometimes brokered fire insurance — get-out-of-hell-free cards — instead of inviting you into God's fullness. I'm sorry we sometimes forgot to exemplify "kingdom" in this world.

I'm sorry if we approached you or didn't approach you based on external criteria like your socioeconomic class, skin color, education level, or any other trait that made you more or less like "us." I'm sorry for the times our message has isolated you; made you feel more judged than forgiven; or offended your family, friends, or people group in a way that didn't reflect the teachings and example of Jesus.

I'm sorry for the times we acted like your mistakes were worse than our own. I'm sorry we failed to realize that life is hard — just generally hard no matter who you are — and that we weren't generous enough with grace and compassion unless it worked to our benefit.

I'm sorry we locked our doors when we drove through your neighborhoods or shirked you when you tried to talk to us in the checkout lines. I'm sorry that we spent more time avoiding you than really getting to know you, that we wrote you off before we even knew your names or stories. That we pretended to understand where you came from, when really we had never bothered to truly listen.

I'm sorry for the times when we acted as if faith and doubt could never coexist, as if it was wrong for you to have questions about why God allowed evil in the world, instead of encouraging you to ask the questions and grow through them. I'm sorry that we acted like there were answers to every question when there are some questions we just can't be sure about, that only God knows the answers to.

I'm sorry we sometimes told you what to believe and how to believe instead of letting you discover and own your journey for yourselves.

I'm sorry we sometimes cared more about whether you came to our church or our choir concert or our youth group or our Bible school than we cared about whether you knew how to live in God's fullness.

After all you may have been through, I understand if you have given up on the people within local churches, but please don't give up on our God. In the times we have made him out to be less than he is, cheapened his church by shaping it via our agenda instead of his, we have committed terrible offenses. Forgive us or don't, but know that in our smartest and most sensible moments, we would forget our pride or our desire to be the "most spiritual" and we would get down on our knees and beg you to reconsider the Savior who is eternally nobler and more just than we are.

You must know that even if you can never respect the church, even if you doubt everything that comes out of our mouths, the one thing that is still true is that Christ wants relationship with you, and therefore opening yourself up to him would be hands-down the best investment you could ever make in your life.

And if you do come to follow Christ, I pray you follow better and more closely than the rest of us have.

Most of all, I'm sorry we haven't apologized more often or sooner.

To the church at large, I'm sorry for the times we saw one Christian or group of Christians fail and assumed the worst of all Christians. I'm sorry that we often put you in the place of Christ, expecting you to be blameless and mistake-free when that was never the identity you were supposed to bear.

I'm sorry observers have failed to appreciate your role in bonding society, in providing not just six weeks of visits to a professional counselor but a lifetime of community with real people. I'm sorry we didn't always understand how you contributed to society's well-being both nationally and internationally. I'm sorry we have mocked you in our comedy sketches, political cartoons, talk shows, and disillusionment-heavy books.

I'm sorry we didn't always honor you like a *Bride* magazine cover girl at the moment she swings open the sanctuary doors to walk down the aisle on life's brightest occasion. We would do well to remember, Church, that this is who you are to our Lord.

We are eternally glad that you exist for the generations before us, for us, and for our children to come. And lastly, don't worry, Church — there are still those of us who will protect you until the last breath.

And to Jesus, our Head, I am so sorry for the times when we heard your clear direction but postponed our obedience to siphon just a little of your glory for ourselves. I'm sorry for not trusting that you alone — if lifted up — draw all people unto yourself more than any plan or strategy that we could contrive. I'm sorry we sometimes tried to operate as a ghostly institution floating around with no head, acting separately from you and by our own power.

I truly regret the times we reduced "faith" to regimented formulas for success. And I'm embarrassed that when our human thinking failed to produce the kind of supernatural results we were looking for, we somehow still blamed you for the deficits. I'm sorry for how we have sometimes abused your freedom and crafted a version of you to suit our own purposes.

I am most sorry for the times when the way I lived as "church" didn't project what you intended, when the Jesus I described flew in the face of your actual persona, when the God I worshiped wasn't really you at all but reflections of you (like success or perfection). I'm sorry for not realizing the satisfaction to be had in being teamed in your mission. I'm sorry for wasting a day, a breath, a dollar, for acting like I had "given my life" when I was actually keeping it for myself.

I know it must seem like I am constantly distracted, that my priorities are misaligned, and that I allow way too many causes to compete for the life that was supposed to be yours. But know that, in the moments when I am sanest, when I am clearest on who I want to be, I want nothing more than to know you. And that I want more moments like that so that tomorrow I will know you and love you even more than I know you and love you today.

You know, of course, that I am not even wise enough to know all the things that we should be sorry for, Jesus. So forgive me, and forgive all of us who call ourselves church, for the times we have both knowingly and unknowingly distanced ourselves from you and for the times we will inevitably err in the future. And thank you for your ongoing patience and investment in helping us grow at our pace and according to our own capacity.

DISCUSSION QUESTIONS

1. Have you ever felt that someone owed you an apology or at least an explanation? Did waiting for that apology prevent you from moving on or developing a forgiving spirit yourself?

2. Which of the apologies that the author made, if any, spoke to your situation best? Had you ever had anyone apologize to you for these sorts of offenses before? Why do you think this happened or did not happen?

3. Have you ever expressed sorrow for what happened in a group situation or for pain caused by someone else? Imagine why this might be healing for both the person expressing the apology and the person receiving it.

KEY IDEAS

◆ Oftentimes our self-defined "need" to be apologized to or declared "right" can cause us to resentfully ask for someone else (whose offense we often believe was greater) to apologize first. This belief that we're entitled to an explanation may be true, but it often prevents us from adopting an attitude of grace.

◆ People are often hurt by church experiences, or unanticipated fallout results due to the ways churches are structured, but often no one takes responsibility for the church's harmful moments. Instead, because we can see the church as a nameless, faceless institution, we all may feel as though it is not our responsibility to do the apologizing for it.

◆ Being generous with grace and opting to express sorrow for the times the church fails to be what God intends for us can be life giving and healing for both the person offering the apology and the person receiving it.

Chapter 14

Love Letter

It may surprise you — sometimes it surprises me — that I am where I am today. That I can still say I love the church. And, after all of this, I believe she deserves one really good love letter. So here goes...

Dear Church,

It is difficult to describe how much I love you, but I once heard Willow Creek pastor Bill Hybels take a pretty good stab at it. Hybels was asked to speak at a church in Canada. Right before he took the stage, a woman from the congregation recounted her broken past — one that was characterized by hurt and disillusionment. Yet her story had the ending of Hybels's dreams: she had been introduced to Jesus by that local church.

The woman's story melted Hybels. In his book *Courageous Leadership*, he describes his internal response to her testimony: "You personify what my life is all about.

I'd have given everything I am and have to hear one story like yours."

By the time he got to the stage, Hybels was an emotional mess. Abandoning his carefully planned speech, he opted to peel back his title and let people see straight into his heart. Right to his love for the church. He said, "Give your life to this.... Give all the money you can give. Give all the service you can give. Give all the prayers you can give. Give whatever you have to give, because for all eternity you'll look back over your shoulder and be glad you did."

Later Hybels attempted to describe the depth of love he has for the church. "I can't count how many times I've fallen on my knees after a ministry event at Willow or elsewhere and said to God, 'Nothing else does this to me. Clearly I was born for this.'"[16]

And you know what, Church? Hybels's love for you does me in every time. When he describes his passion for local churches, every church-related moment of my lifetime swells to my memory and sends my heart into overdrive. I can't agree with him more. Being a member of your crew has been the premier privilege of my life as well. It's been that way as far back as I can remember.

So I write you, Church, because despite your flaws and despite my affair with disillusionment, I love you. Many of my peers love you too.

I love you because you are brilliant. You started out as this fragile little group of marginalized disciples that almost no one thought would succeed. Yet in a dot-com-like explosion, you emerged on the global scene as a force to be reckoned with. Google and eBay have nothing on you, Church.

I love you, Church, because you're accessible. From Philip's run-in with the Ethiopian to Peter's dream of animals falling from heaven, you refused to limit yourself to just one group of people. Now missionaries from every country catapult themselves all over the world and back again just to make sure every tribe on the planet gets a personal invitation to join you. Sure, there are some barriers remaining, but I'm putting my money on you, Church. Forget McDonald's, you've served billions upon billions.

I love you, Church, because you're consistent. Dark Ages? You were there. Renaissance? You were there too. Enlightenment, modern, postmodern. There, there, and there. The US government may be determined to separate religion and the state, Church, but they've never figured out a way to teach history without mentioning you.

I love you, Church, because you take action. Despite entertaining Easter cantatas and mouthwatering potluck dishes, you aren't interested in the hotel business where people rent your rooms just to rest in comfort. No. You manage to punt people out into the community, as if you had forgotten that you ever had walls to keep them in. You remind them, generation after generation, that Jesus' favorite verb was *go*.

I love you, Church, because you're learning from your mistakes. Despite your role in the Crusades, your part in the abuse of Native Americans, your failure to address American slavery, or your exclusion of those unlike your members, you kept trodding along until there were enough numbers among you to stand up for what was right. Despite cults who poisoned people with Kool-Aid, men who locked their followers in camps, and evangelists who slept around when the cameras weren't on, you carried your shame and regret without losing the ability to hold your head high.

I love you because you are tough. Fear could not bust up the commitment of your leaders. Lock them in prison? They'll write half the New Testament. Banish them to an island? They'll write the grand finale to the world's bestseller. Crucify them upside down? Their examples will become the rock on which your future is built. Catacombs, hostile natives, guillotines, or guns to the head — the rusty, prickly gates of hell have heaved with all their force. But through the help of Jesus, your Head, you slammed shut the gates, proving again and again that hell would never prevail against you.

I love you, Church, because you're resilient. You've been portrayed from so many unflattering angles. Movies offer fanatical Christian characters trying to blow up government projects. TV shows present sweaty choir-robed mobs engaging in something akin to a pep assembly for exorcists. Comedians do gigs as kneesock-wearing Sunday school teachers with nasally voices and enormous bifocals. You've been laughed at, accused, ignored, and misused. But you always get up the next morning ready to press on toward the mark.

I love you, Church, because you're never satisfied with where you are. You revamp your music from psalms to chants to hymns to choruses. You move from contemporary to praise and worship ... and then, ironically, back to chants again. You always push yourself, examine yourself, try to improve yourself from generation to generation. I can't wait to see what you become in our generation and beyond.

I think more than anything, Church, I love you because of your flexibility. You started simple, known as little more than a group of friends who lived, ate, and prayed together. You could have patented this idea, stamped this one model as *the* model — the only one you officially endorsed. Yet you let guys like Paul carry you around and disperse you all over the place. In Antioch, Iconium, Lystra, and Derbe. In prisons, synagogues, two-story houses, and courtrooms. You let common laborers such as Aquila and Priscilla conduct undercover church while doing everyday tasks like building tents. You took up root in the houses of ordinary people in Corinth, Galatia, Ephesus, Philippi, Colossae — I could go on.

You met in stone buildings with columns and stained glass where rabbis, monks, nuns, popes, and priests served. You moved into brick buildings with high steeples and large wooden crosses. You lent yourself to vacation Bible schools, revivals, backyard Bible clubs, workshops, and conferences.

You exploded into buildings ten times the size of anything you'd lived in before, with huge digital screens and surround-sound stereo. You housed cutting-edge worship and emergent experiences right across the street from ones that practiced liturgical prayer and formal sacraments. You split yourself into cells, emergent villages, and then back to house churches. You hung out at faith-based nonprofits, coffeehouses, bars, and restaurants. And you topped it all off by becoming the world's first international corporation, popping up in cities, villages, and remote tribal outposts across the globe.

And if all of this were not enough, this part is hands-down what made me fall in love with you in the first place: you defied logic by transcending physical space. You showed the world that you didn't need steeples or crosses or truckloads of bricks. You set up residence in community itself, presenting yourself in the sometimes buildingless "togetherness" of the Twelve and those who came after them. You *are* the community, even when the community only boasts two or three people.

I love you because I am part of you. Because when my friends and I are teamed in Christ's mission, we are you.

So I write — first and foremost — because I love you.

I love you still. In fact, I somehow think I love you more.

There is something powerful about realizing that a person or institution is not perfect and loving them anyway. Sometimes love is all the reason a person needs to stay in contact. So I leave you with this final message: I love you.

In sickness and in health, I love you.

DISCUSSION QUESTIONS

1. If you had to stop right now and write a love letter to your local church (or the global one), could you do it? Explain.
2. If it would be difficult to write a love letter, is it because there is nothing to love, or because you've closed off space

in your heart due to hurt and disillusionment? What might you do to release any lingering hurt or disappointment with the church and allow yourself to appreciate the positive contributions it has made and can make in your life?

3. If you would find it easy to write a love letter, how do you maintain a positive concept of the church while still acknowledging its flaws? Was there a stage of life when you grappled with forgiving your church? How did you get out of that stage?

4. If you don't feel that you can write a love letter to your local church, could you manage one for the global version? Are there Christians outside of your church who have influenced your life for the positive?

5. Share some of the things you love most about the church (be it local or global). List as many positives as you can. You may even want to compose your own letter to express your love for the community of people who follow Jesus in this world.

KEY IDEA

◆ Although church life is marked with hardship, that does not necessarily rule out the presence of deep, enduring love. Perhaps it is the journey through hardship, in fact, that strengthens our love for the church the most.

Afterword:
Where I Am Now

Confession: Updating a book you wrote in the throes of disillusionment when you were twenty-three years old is an ironic, awkward task.

For good reason.

Today, eleven years after I started writing the first edition of this book and seven years after it was first released, one major thing has changed: *I am no longer disillusioned with the church.*

I am not suggesting that my life and faith are seamless or pretending that this season of life is absent of disappointment and curveballs. Rather, in those disappointments, my conscience is absent of angst. I still grieve in bits and pieces the many ways the church of today falls short of what it could be. But I have accepted some things that were important for framing life with realistic expectations. The world and the church are messy arenas. And when you add me to either, I bring even more mess to them.

Even though I never would have expected such healing was possible way back when, I am so far removed from the original book's content that it is a challenge to climb back into my former mind-set that was once so consumed with angst over organized religion. My life and my feelings about church have come to such a different place that when I revisit those days now, it almost seems as though I am telling a story about someone else altogether.

And so, while some have mistakenly labeled me as antichurch because I wrote about disillusionment, I actually value church more today than in any other period of my life. I have found a new rhythm of faith, where church is still central to my Christian experience. Over time though, I have learned to ground my identity in Christ and in his timeless, global church more than I idealize any one local church. This has provided steady ground to experience community without being so sidelined when flaws and dysfunction surface.

And not only do I still love church, but I've actually had the opportunity to share the content of *Dear Church*, the original version of this book, with nearly every church I've been a part of — my dad's current church, his previous church from my childhood, the church where I was on staff, even my college chapel services.

In the end, I have no doubt disillusionment served my life well. I desperately needed to move away from false impressions of reality to a healthier, more mature view of what it means to be part of the church. I hope the healing I've found brings you some small slice of hope to help you carry on so that one day you too will be amazed at how long it has been since you moved beyond the broken church.

Beyond the Broken Church

In the ten or so years since I first began writing the original version of this book, which was formerly titled *Dear Church: Letters from a Disillusioned Generation*, I've had the chance to speak to and learn from people across the country about disillusionment and the church.

So many times, as I have read emails from readers or gathered with pastors, denominational leaders, or the disillusioned themselves, some new conversation or piece of wisdom has emerged that I wished I could capture and share with my readers. I've tried to collect some of that conversation in the appendices that follow.

Appendix A: *Resources for the Disillusioned*

Appendix B: *Resources for the Local Pastor or Church Staff Who Serve the Disillusioned*

Appendix C: *Resources for Denominational Leaders*

Appendix D: *Resources for Parents and Family Members of the Disillusioned*

Appendix E: *Fifty Things I've Learned about Forgiveness*

Appendix F: *Resources for Learning More about Disillusionment*

Appendix A:
Resources
for the Disillusioned

I wish I had videos of the discussions that took place as I presented my experiences during the years after the release of *Dear Church*, so that you might observe the wonderful synergy and wisdom that came out of these events. Since I didn't have the benefit of a personal camera crew, however, on the following pages I have tried to capture some of the questions and discussion points that were commonly raised.

Are you still disillusioned?

There are some things I will always be a little bit frustrated by. I'm frustrated, for example, about the lack of authenticity I sometimes see in church culture. I'm frustrated when too much "celebrity" creeps into Christians' public platforms. I'm frustrated by abuses of power, by failure to welcome diverse people groups, by churches investing more time, money, and energy in buildings than in building relationships with the people outside of them.

But I think some ongoing tension is okay because it keeps us from forgetting and from becoming comfortable with harmful acts. The enduring uncomfortableness keeps us trying to envision a better way and working toward solutions. The world is too marked by suffering and oppression and evil for us to afford to be neutral.

There are other kinds of disillusionment — disillusionment with specific people, situations, or events — that I've been able to shake free of almost completely. While I'll probably always carry the memory of the pain and the lessons learned from those bad stretches in my church history, as I release things I am not in control of, as I learn not to recycle bad feelings from past difficulties, and as I work at both apologizing and forgiving, I become free.

You don't talk about the people who were responsible for your disillusionment much.

That's not true. I actually do talk about the person most responsible for my disillusionment — because that person is me.

The older I get, the better I get at not letting negative experiences consume me or my time and energy. When something tragic first happens, it can send me reeling. And the initial emotional fallout may be prompted by another person's actions. But after that, whether I wake up the next day or the day after that and keep revisiting the same bad experiences and cycling through the same painful emotions is up to me. It's no longer someone else's fault. Other people can't climb inside my brain and tell me what to obsess over when I'm falling asleep at night. That's my choice. And I try (sometimes unsuccessfully) not to project responsibility for my emotions on other people anymore but to acknowledge that the person most responsible for my disillusionment is me.

I do get what you're saying though: I haven't said much about the other people involved in my story. That's on purpose. I've tried not to publicly draw attention to people who were a part of my most difficult faith experiences. Even those who contribute to our pain are human beings — they are dearly loved fathers, mothers, sons, daughters, husbands, or wives to someone. And God is still at work wanting good for all of them. So sometimes, even though we — as free Americans — have the right to write about anything we want and to broadcast others' dirty laundry to sell books or validate our stories, it is wiser to lay down that right in deference to our love for those involved and in deference to the good we know God still wants to bring about for every human being involved.

Have you ever confronted people who were involved in your painful experiences?

Definitely. Sometimes it went well, other times not so well. More often than not, I would say the initial conversations fell short of my hopes for them and were tough to bear. But in the months and years to come, a lot of emotion faded and minds cleared and perspective dawned, both for me and for other parties — and almost all my relationships with people involved in my story are better than they used to be. Some relationships are stronger because of what we've walked through. And some have come so full circle that I feel as though I've experienced a miracle.

Looking back, if I could do it over, I would try to humanize more the people who were part of the difficult moments. I would try to remind myself that they weren't monsters who woke up in the morning plotting to make my life miserable or to hurt people in the name of Christ. They were, instead, equally broken people, with their own private yearnings and disappointments, who were trying to find their way just as I was — and sometimes made mistakes, just as I did, along the way.

When you finally get the chance to confront someone, unleashing everything at once can be a huge temptation. You may want to vent and give a full dissertation on their history of flaws. But that almost never helps. And in a lot of cases, at least for me, when I released some diatribe, it actually revealed my arrogance. Although I was trying to stand for what was right, I often took that opportunity too far and showed a lot of pride in believing I somehow was one of the only ones who could see the situation and the simple solution so easily.

Yes, I spent too much time vilifying people then and not enough time being gracious. When we monsterize people, we form hypotheses about them — this person doesn't care about others, for example — and then we watch their lives and try to collect evidence to support our hypotheses. But when we do this, we filter out all of the good and home in on the bad. The villain maker, a lot of times, is us and not them.

How do you protect against disillusionment now?

Well, there's no foolproof protection for disillusionment. We live in an imperfect world, so we will never be immune to suffering. But in addition to learning to manage my emotions better, one major thing that helps me avoid or lessen some tension is noticing earlier when I am in a situation that isn't serving me or other people well.

When I was younger, I went through times when I was very frustrated that I could not continue to experience good — or contribute good — in the context I was in. Out of a desire to "never give up," I sometimes stayed too embroiled in situations that tempted me to become more and more bitter. And often I didn't realize I needed to separate myself from the situation until I'd already become high maintenance, struggling to manage my emotions and letting my frustrations spiral beyond what was helpful.

Today I am a lot better at avoiding situations that create this kind of emotional tension. But I still run into frustrations sometimes that prompt emotion that surprises me. The difference now is that I am much quicker to recognize a misfit, to realize when my own desires for a situation are different than those of other parties, to understand when things are outside of my control. I am much quicker to reduce my interactions with people or situations that feel harmful or unjust and more confident to believe I can still stay committed to the people and "never give up" on them even if I'm not interacting with them as much as I used to. Sometimes space is a powerful tool for healing.

Also — and this is a shameless plug — I collected in a book all the wisdom I've been accumulating (mostly from other people) these last ten or fifteen years for people who are facing disillusionment. It's called

The Well-Balanced World Changer: A Field Guide for Staying Sane While Doing Good.[17]

How do you look at church now?

In many ways, I look at the church just as I always did — as a group of people with whom I can experience community and learn about and worship God. But I am less likely to idolize any local church, to brag about it, or to see it as the only or superior source of spiritual guidance. And although I still feel ownership and membership in the local church, I try to stake my identity not in a specific building, group of people, or denomination but rather in being a follower of Jesus. I work harder to recognize that I am teamed with all people who claim to follow Christ whether they attend my local church or not.

I do still attend church, and in seasons when it makes sense with my writing, speaking, and parenting obligations, I try to serve in or volunteer for my local congregation. I have yet to find the same kind of belonging in the local church I felt prior to becoming disillusioned with it, but I experience deep belonging with many believers who are part of the church — both the local one and the global version. With each passing year, however, I seem to feel more inspired and hopeful about being committed to and involved in the church. For now, I find myself content with contributing in nonleadership roles, serving behind the scenes in areas like the nursery, as opposed to taking more spotlighted positions, speaking from the stage, which might have been more typical of me in the past. I'm as excited about being the church — alongside a planet of other followers of Christ — as I have ever been.

I try to encourage others not to sever ties with all expressions of church. I don't think this is responsible. We can't justify dividing from those who speak in Jesus' name and dividing the church's resources. I won't do it.

TEN SIGNS YOUR DISILLUSIONMENT MAY BE TURNING INTO DEPRESSION AND IT MAY BE TIME TO SEEK PROFESSIONAL COUNSELING

1. You feel unmotivated, particularly when it comes to participating in church or hanging out with people involved in your current conflict. You decline offers to hang out at the last minute, show up late, and leave early. You experience more boredom and apathy than usual and have difficulty concentrating on tasks at hand or making even routine decisions.

2. You find yourself delivering more and more sarcastic and cynical remarks about life in general, but particularly about your church or faith experience. You're angry enough that you almost enjoy biting humor, even at the expense of others, and you sometimes see your bitter commentary as clever and admirable.

3. You overcompensate for your internal tension or the tension between others. This displays itself in fake cheerfulness, excessive politeness, or avoidance of conflict.

4. Your sleep is disrupted. You spend a lot of time processing and reprocessing your disappointments or conflicts as you lie in bed. You can't sleep, are tired and fatigued even when you do sleep, and may even have bad dreams.

5. Your eating patterns are skewed. You don't feel hungry due to stress making you feel sick, or you overeat to drown the pain.

6. Your body is acting up. You find yourself sighing frequently, your muscles feel tense (back, neck, stomach), you have headaches, and you are quicker to become irritable, to raise your voice, or to cry. You are restless; you pace in circles, wring your hands, or have trouble sitting still.

7. You kill time with hours of escapist activity, such as surfing the Internet, watching entire seasons of television shows in one day, overworking yourself, or sleeping, just so you will not have

to think about or feel any negative emotions related to your challenges.

8. Your frustrations feel difficult enough and present enough that they interfere with your normal routines.

9. You think in extremes, going from blaming others to blaming yourself; from determining to resolve the situation at all costs to considering moving across the country to get away from the source of your frustrations.

10. You feel anxious and stressed more than you feel normal. Even things that used to be easy for you feel troubling or intimidating now.

TEN WAYS TO HELP YOURSELF LET IT GO

1. Know your triggers.

Think about previous emotional cycles you've walked through, and try to determine what sorts of things tend to send you spiraling into negativity. Figure out what triggers divert your mood, and determine to take an alternative course of action, such as going for a run or doing a hobby you enjoy. Make a rule to wait until you are calm to confront anyone. Never send an email or leave a voice mail while experiencing strong emotion.

2. Identify the fears or deficits behind your emotions.

Strong displays of emotion are often signs that you feel your support is lacking, your needs are not being met, or you are being devalued. Try to figure out what the underlying need is behind your emotions, and seek other ways to fill that need. Hang out with friends to boost your feelings of support. Or send a thank-you card that shows appreciation so you can feel good about investing in another worthwhile relationship.

3. Limit your obsession.

Set a time limit, such as five minutes, for how much you allow yourself to think or analyze the past each day. Then stick to it. After you've rehashed it for a minute aloud or in your head, force yourself to change the subject. Cut off lengthy attempts to analyze, theorize, intellectualize, and otherwise dwell on what has happened. Remind yourself that going on and on about it won't solve the problem but will only allow the problem to consume even more of your life, making the cost to you more than it already is.

4. Search for balance.

Try to weed out extreme and exaggerative words like *always* and *never*. And balance each negative statement that comes out of your mouth, not just to be fair to the listener but to force yourself to see multiple perspectives. "He doesn't care who he hurts in his climb to the top" becomes "He doesn't care who he hurts in his climb to the top, or ... well, maybe he does. I know he loves his kids, and he has been kind to me a number of times. It just seems like he is being selfish right now."

5. Believe in the long-term results of doing what is right.

If you act appropriately, even when others do not, over time your self-control to act aboveboard will stand out and earn you credibility. You might feel like unloading on someone or returning evil for evil, but don't give in to your feelings. They're temporary. Muster the willpower to do the right thing one day at a time, and eventually those right actions will become habit. When you refuse to add fuel to the fire and you don't give ammunition to a person you're in conflict with, you pave the way for more peace down the road. Trust that God desires to work things together for good for you and all those involved (Romans 8:28).

6. Take a break.

Step away from ministry commitments or stop attending services for a short, limited amount of time (for example, one month) while you heal. Perhaps find a small group you can attend at another church or a sermon series you can listen to online to stay mentally engaged in the work of the church while removing yourself from the painful scenario in order to become more objective.

7. Take care of yourself.

You will feel better and will deal better with emotions when you have slept and eaten enough, when you are exercising, and when you are spending time with people you enjoy and taking the time to participate in hobbies and activities that bring you pleasure.

8. Go around dead ends.

Whenever you hit a dead end and you can't resolve your differences, determine to make maintaining the relationship more important than being declared right. You don't have to agree on any of your concerns to go on valuing this person and believing in what God is stirring in his or her life.

9. Keep revisiting your strongest values.

You probably believe that reconciliation is better than conflict, that forgiveness is better than resentment. Continue to reinforce your beliefs by taking a few minutes to recenter yourself in reflection or prayer or by placing some kind of reminders in your environment.

10. Intentionally practice gratitude.

Take the time to pause and scan your environment for things you can be grateful for. Are you generally physically healthy? Do you have reliable shelter and enough to eat? Are you living in an area that is free of civil war and immediate military threat? Are there people in your life who have been good to you? Have you had the opportunities to be educated or otherwise mentored so that you are better prepared than some to face the challenges at hand? "Whatever is true, whatever is noble, whatever is right, whatever is pure, whatever is lovely, whatever is admirable ... think about such things" (Philippians 4:8).

Appendix B:

Resources for the Local Pastor
or Church Staff Who Serve
the Disillusioned

***Our church has lost a lot of people, particularly young people,
without explanation. Is this likely a sign of disillusionment
impacting our congregation?***

It might be. Disillusionment, at some level — small or large — is likely
always impacting some in our congregations, but we rarely know about it.

There are likely a variety of explanations for why people have left,
some of which may involve tension with the church and some of which
likely have nothing to do with it. To learn more about why people are
breaking connection, you might try putting an informal exit survey into
place. I recommend following up in person to check on former attendees
after they have been absent for a month or longer. But after a person or
family has obviously stopped attending (for example, after they've been
gone for several months), you might send them a link to a digital survey
that they can choose to take anonymously if they please. Ask people if
there is anything the church can do to offer support if they are experiencing hardship or illness. Ask if they have any concerns they would like to
talk to a staff person about; or if they don't want to talk in person, ask
them to express their concerns in the survey.

Without some way of gathering data, we can only make assumptions about why people are leaving, and this may lead us to put our energies toward ineffective changes.

When the church does hit a rough time, the circumstances may involve personal and highly sensitive information. Should a church share this sort of drama with the church?

If you want your church people to respect your voice and to feel as if they have been honored as well, it is incredibly important to be authentic about times of struggle. If the church runs into financial hardship or an obvious leadership failure, for example, it is not wise to go into gory detail about what has gone down. But saying nothing can make volunteers who feel ownership — like they are high stakes investors in the church — feel disrespected and untrusted, and it can also lead to widespread speculation about what happened that ends up being more harmful than the actual mishap. In most cases, it makes sense for the person who failed and the church leadership to decide together about what information should be released.

Even if there are details about the situation that should be kept private in order to protect the families of those involved, it can be sufficiently helpful to simply acknowledge the rough times by saying something like this: "This has been a hard week around here. We're losing a staff person, and that is never easy. Some of the reasons the person is leaving are personal, and we're not going to talk about the situation from the public stage because we know none of us would want our sensitive situations aired in public. But we wanted to stress that this has been a tough time, and we don't want to be one of those churches who make it tougher by gossiping or speculating. So we want to encourage you to pray for this staff member, and if you feel concern for him, reach out to him and express your love and thanks for the investment he has made here. We want to join together, even in hard times, in expressing goodwill to this person and also in wishing him and the church the best transition possible and a healthy, life-giving future."

There is nothing you can do to prevent all gossip, of course, but placing the responsibility on people to continue in relationship with the offending party rather than disconnecting from him or her and trying to pry information from others is often a step in the right direction.

You talk about how disillusionment is often an invisible disease and how people of faith are often good at hiding their concerns. How then can we proactively offer support to those who need it?

First, be authentic in known times of conflict or division. Don't ignore it; lead people through it. Help them think about what a wise and God-honoring response to the situation would be. And help them identify what kind of responses might be harmful as well.

Second, if you've experienced a severe loss of some kind — perhaps, for example, there has been a public scandal in the church body that has hit the newspapers — you may want to host some sort of special reconciliation service where you encourage people to seek God's healing for the church. This might include an encouraging word and a call to persevere from a pastor or elder; worship songs that focus on trusting God, finding hope, and overcoming obstacles; and open opportunity for prayer or counseling. It might also include some sort of gathering where people express (perhaps on paper) and release anger or frustrations or worries to God or where they do something practical (such as sign a giant banner or record videos) to express love and support for someone who is struggling.

Third, come up with a process for congregation members or regular attendees to offer feedback, and make sure the congregation knows about it. It might include an open invitation to meet with a pastor or elder to discuss concerns, a yearly feedback meeting where people can offer insights, or an email address or web form where they are encouraged to submit feedback. Having the opportunity to communicate one's concerns along the way is one small way that we can help prevent negative feelings from building up or becoming exaggerated if left unresolved.

Fourth, pastors can offer in a sermon series, or in a small group curriculum, material that builds people's expectations that even as people of faith, we will encounter hardships. Stress how that includes struggle and tension with even our church or church community. The pastor can offer ideas to keep in mind when facing difficulties and thoughts about how to manage our emotions well and make responsible choices while still being up front and honest.

Fifth, churches can provide opportunities to read through this book — or a similar book that discusses disillusionment — in a small group or with a staff member on a lunch hour, for example. Create a safe place to discuss concerns and to talk about how to resolve tensions with church members, the local congregation, and any troubling public or global expressions of Christianity.

Lastly, make supportive resources available. Offer prayer and counseling support for those who are especially frustrated. Purchase a handful of books about overcoming frustration and/or collect CDs or links to sermons about dealing with suffering, and publicize that they are available to be borrowed free of charge. Perhaps have Scripture or a handout available for easy pickup at your information table, labeling it with something like "Are You Struggling with Church?" and notifying the reader of your church's opportunities to dialogue about their concerns.

What should church leaders do if the disillusioned leave? Even if we know they are disillusioned, it seems like we might be the last people they want to talk to about it.

It's true; for some, church leaders may be the last people they'd want to talk to, but I happen to think that just as often, you're likely the *first* person they'd like to talk to about their situation. After all, you may be the person who can do the most about it — the person who has enough information to answer their questions about the church or the person who has the influence to draw attention to an area that could be improved.

Here's what I'd suggest. Invite the person to coffee at a local public coffeehouse (not at the church, where it might be perceived as your home turf). Presuming it is true, tell her you've been thinking about her and that you personally wanted to connect with her to see how she is doing.

See what she offers when you ask open-ended questions like "How have you been?," "How's work?," and so on. If she broaches the subject of disillusionment, listen to everything she has to say and try to focus on acknowledging that she feels hurt (even if you don't understand it) and expressing sorrow that some part of her church experience has been harmful. Stress that you hope she knows how much you value her and want her around.

If she doesn't bring up any frustrations, it's possible that either she doesn't have any or she isn't comfortable or ready to talk about them. If this is the case, and if you know her well, you might feel that it is appropriate to ask, "Is everything going okay? Any concerns?" or to just state plainly, "Look, I want to be up front with you. I'm worried that something is wrong and that there is some sort of tension between you and the church. You don't have to talk about it, but if you want to, I'd love to listen."

If you do not know the person well and you sense she doesn't want to open up right then, let this initial meeting close casually. Be positive and upbeat as you part ways. If you can do so genuinely, name things you appreciate about her and wish her the best in her endeavors. Say something like, "I'm always glad to see you. Let's keep in touch. And call me if you need anything." Maybe a day or two later, follow up with a text message, email, Facebook post, or even a handwritten postcard saying you enjoyed meeting with her and you hope to see her again soon.

I'm amazed at how many leaders have told me that their successes in helping frustrated people reconcile with the church started with making a simple, inexpensive gesture indicating that they still cared.

If the conversation does turn into a venting session, you might be able to help the person by saying something to help her focus and help you identify what is really the central issue, such as, "It sounds like all of this weighs heavily on you. Do you think you could narrow your frustrations down to one big thing you think needs improvement?" This might be a helpful time to suggest she talk to someone more directly related to her issue, to offer to loan or give her resources you think would be helpful, or — and this may be the best idea yet — to offer to help her figure out a way that she can be part of the solution by supporting or starting a new ministry or effort.

Finally, if the conversation ends without any resolution (which is probably a realistic expectation to have going into it), predetermine to be okay with this. Remind yourself this isn't the only time you will have to follow up with this person, and you aren't the only person God will send to encourage and support her going forward. Instead, show that you care about her and would like to stay in contact even if she chooses not to attend, and encourage her to take care of herself physically and spiritually in the meantime.

HOT-BUTTON ISSUES REPORTED BY THE DISILLUSIONED

Some disillusioned people have indicated they feel uncomfortable with the following ideas. Even if you do not agree with those who are currently frustrated with their church experience, it might be helpful to read through them and think about why these people might feel as they do. Sometimes if you can't come to agreement on particulars, the next best thing you can do is to seek to be a friend and understand people as well as you can.

- Churches who pressure participants to raise their hands, engage in clap offerings, or offer other prompted responses throughout the services. (They often don't mind that the option is mentioned, but they don't like to be repeatedly asked about it.) They like the freedom to engage God in whatever way feels natural to them — but no less actively — than the people onstage.

- Churches whose teams try to overpolish the worship services. They appreciate the hard work that goes into developing a few good song sets and well-thought-out, well-presented sermons, but they don't like to feel nervous as if they're at an important dinner for dignitaries that is being hosted by a controlling, type A leader. They don't want to see people sweating bullets over a slightly squeaky microphone or a typo on the big screen. *When did church become so serious and pressured?* they want to know. *This isn't making a presentation to Congress or performing on* American Idol. *It's spending time with a God who already loves us side by side with other normal, flawed people we're sharing life with. What's with all the show?*

- Churches whose leaders come down hard on certain sins but allow other ones to run rampant — even in their own lives. (When was the last time we became publicly judgmental about Deacon Donutlover's gut or Molly the nursery coordinator's ongoing penchant for gossip, for example?)

- Churches that inflate attendance numbers or take every opportunity to toss them out. Same goes for bragging about other church "achievements." (They are glad you have something to celebrate, but there are still times when a little old-school "to God be the glory" might be in order.)

- Churches that are heavy on secrecy. (It is specifically when questions are discouraged that people feel a need to ask the most questions.)

- Churches whose leaders pretend to get along onstage — singing and smiling at each other as the service unfolds — only to boldly gossip about each other when the spotlight goes down.

- Churches whose onstage dress code seems to keep high-end designer clothing stores in business. To some this feels like elitism or exclusion. (When Abercrombie starts sending you endorsement checks, it might be time for a change ... of clothes.)

• Churches that go overboard on the "experiential" or "high-tech" factor. (If the fire department shows up for weekly false alarms, that might be a sign you have a few too many candles onstage — no matter how "cool" they are.)

• Churches that are obsessed with being on top of the "latest" — whether it be technology, music, books, or lingo. (While the cutting edge may *seem* cool, our parents taught us to be careful around sharp blades.)

TEN THINGS THE DISILLUSIONED DON'T WANT CHURCHES TO USE TO JUDGE SPIRITUAL HEALTH

1. How regularly a person volunteers within the church infrastructure. (Hint: They think it might be just as or more mission aligned to serve those *outside* the church.)

2. Whether their church is huge or growing by leaps and bounds.

3. How "entertaining" the church service or other programs are.

4. Whether the church gets a lot of regional or national attention or is often featured in the media.

5. Whether the church's staff write books or record albums or have thousands of social media followers.

6. Whether they're at the church every time the doors are open.

7. Whether they're trying to attain the highest levels of leadership within the church system.

8. Whether they come to the faith through a repeat-after-me prayer (that's not in the Bible and that Jesus never employed) or through some other more organic instance of stumbling into God and beginning to believe.

9. Whether they follow the normalized path to success in our culture (for example, whether they go to college or join the rat race or marry or buy a home).
10. Whether they image manage (by hiding their flaws and doubts, for example) enough to keep everyone comfortable.

Some of the disillusioned also feel that too many unhealthy things have crept into how we define and experience (and even mandate!) church. They are often anxious to get back to brass tacks, to think about what the enduring qualities are that need to be present for a group of people to seek God as a community of friends.

They ask us to examine which, if any, of the following are necessary or helpful:

- an artistic facility
- a twenty- to thirty-minute sermon
- a passed-around offering
- baptisteries
- refreshments in the lobby
- high-tech lighting
- coffeehouses or other alternative locations
- steeples
- digital screens
- high ceilings
- guitars and saxophones
- the American or Christian flags
- seminaries
- pulpits
- denominations
- membership
- bulletins
- websites
- a one-hour service
- a video projector
- individual children's classes divided by grade
- candles
- a constant supply of Christian literature
- stages
- pews and/or rows/circles of chairs
- choirs and/or worship teams
- praying to close a service
- a 9:30 or 11:00 a.m. Sunday time slot
- stained-glass windows
- a Communion table with an open Bible
- stereo sound systems

- large wooden crosses
- pianos and organs
- announcements
- a visitors' or information table
- altars
- a dress code
- nondenominations
- clap offerings
- mass email lists
- altar calls
- a worship leader
- small groups
- the ability to perform weddings
- nonprofit status
- the ability to perform funerals

TWELVE THINGS YOU WANT TO KNOW ABOUT YOUNG PEOPLE AND THE CHURCH

Older twentysomethings and thirtysomethings have been tagged Generation X, while younger twentysomethings have been lumped into Generation Y or Z. You may also know them as baby busters, echo boomers, or millennials.

Not all generational nicknames are positive. Some people call young people *kiddults, twixters,* or *adultolescents* — none of which strikes me as a compliment. They've also been dubbed the Slacker Generation, the "Me" Generation, and in the worst of times, the "Me! Me! Me!" Generation.

The young, of course, tend to prefer the more favorable reviews, like Neil Howe and William Strauss's description in *Millennials Rising: The Next Generation,* in which they say young people are "unlike any other youth generation in living memory."[18]

Despite other people's penchant for nicknaming the young, most young adults are quick to shrug off the titles. Robert Webber, author of *Younger Evangelicals,* was right when he pointed out that young believers don't like being labeled.[19]

1. Young people redefine the word family.

Perhaps all those feel-good family talks on *Growing Pains* and *Full House* paid off, because the young have emerged as "family people." In 2002

University of Maryland psychologist Jeffrey Jensen Arnett told *Newsweek*, "We are seeing a closer relationship between generations than we have seen since World War II.... Young people genuinely like and respect their parents."[20]

Similarly, in 2009 LifeWay Research's survey of 1,200 millennials found young people value family above all else. Sixty-one percent of millennials place family at the top of their priority lists, followed by friends (25 percent), education (17 percent), careers/jobs (16 percent), spouses/partners (13 percent), and spirituality/religion (13 percent).

"Millennials are committed to family above other priorities, even though many are waiting to start their own families," said Thom Rainer, president of LifeWay Christian Resources. "To minister effectively, the church should tap into this priority among Millennials. Churches with a strong understanding and sense of family will be able to more easily reach Millennials. I expect that ministries that cross generations — such as older adults mentoring young adults — could be highly effective in connecting Millennials to Jesus."[21]

Of course, young adults' view of family life might be a bit more inclusive than that of generations past, perhaps because they experienced an unprecedented breakdown of the traditional nuclear family. Only about six in ten were raised by both parents,[22] which means many of them were raised in blended households where they lived with stepparents, stepbrothers and stepsisters, and sometimes half siblings. Survival of the fittest demanded that their generation widen their definition of family to include some who were not genetically related.

As a result, some young people may have generated their own philosophy of family. They realized that "family" was more about commitment and state of heart than genetic coding. Thus, they began expanding their "families," building an intimate support group from any number of friends and acquaintances. Often they invited these perceived "outsiders" into the rawness of their lives, including the low points and breakdowns formerly reserved only for the genetic family behind closed doors.

This philosophy of family may make young people especially big believers in spiritual and church family based on sharing a mutual faith in Christ. But it may also make them especially prone to disappointment when these much-loved church family members let them down.

2. Young people are comfortable with competing schools of thought.

Thanks to immense technological breakthroughs, today's young adults have grown up in a "both-and" era. They can get the dinner dishes done *and* still make it to the movie on time, thanks to dishwashers — not to mention on-demand movie streaming. They can have sex *and* still have reasonable assurance they won't get pregnant, thanks to birth control. And they can overeat *and* lose the pounds, thanks to weight-loss drugs and surgeries. Even more obviously, thanks to the Internet and smartphones, they can shop, exercise, clean, or drive without losing touch with their friends.

To both their benefit and detriment, their fast-paced culture has seen few limits that innovations cannot stretch. As a result, young people have not been forced to make as many choices as their predecessors have. Hence, it only follows that they feel that they can have "both-and" in other areas as well. Politically, for example, a 2011 Pew Research study found that "a growing number of Americans are choosing not to identify with either political party, and the center of the political spectrum is increasingly diverse. Rather than being moderate, many of these independents hold extremely strong ideological positions on issues such as the role of government, immigration, the environment, and social issues. But they combine these views in ways that defy liberal or conservative orthodoxy."[23] Younger Americans' real loyalty, then, doesn't seem to lie with a party as much as it lies with an ideal. Young people lean toward humanitarian issues regardless of political affiliation.

This "both-and" mentality plays out socially, educationally, and even spiritually. Young people feel like they can save the world and still goof off with friends, use five-syllable words and still enjoy the world's stupidest movies, and live their faith in a way that can be both academically credible and emotionally viable, doctrinally sound and relationally intelligent.

3. Young people feel connected to their surroundings.

With the dawn of the computer age, some experts predicted that social networks and other technology would diminish younger generations' real-life relationships. However, as young people adapted to our faster and more efficient society, their technology seemed to supplement rather than destroy their real-life relationships. Not only do they hang out with their friends in person, but thanks to smartphones, texts, and social networks, they also talk to them more frequently in between face-to-face encounters. And even if their friends move or travel to the other side of the country or the other side of the world, they still can stay connected through Skype, Google+, and other free, Internet-based communication platforms. Their sense of increased connection isn't just limited to communication with their friends either. Because young people's education included curriculum that focused on environmental, social, and political issues, they have learned to appreciate the invisible cords that attach us all. As follows, studies have suggested young people are more socially compassionate, more community oriented, and more likely to be civically involved or to do activist work.[24]

Rather than focusing solely on their individuality, young adults have come to value the connection between all the components of our communities (traffic, trees, homes, businesses, etc.). Consequently, if a school is not educating its students, if law enforcement turn their heads at crime, if manufacturers dump waste into rivers, young adults feel affected because the economy, safety, and health of their community are affected.

We applaud scholars like Gerald Schlabach, author of *And Who Is My Neighbor?*, who were advocating the value of community before young people arrived on the planet. As Schlabach says, "Individualism only deepens human poverty."[25]

4. Young people don't see money as a trustworthy indicator of success.

In a society whose billboards advertise quick divorces for $99 or less, it should come as no surprise that money is the number-one factor cited in the breakup of most marriages. Besides sometimes claiming young people's parents' marriages, money — or the pursuit of it — occasionally claimed their parents themselves. Overtime became the kidnapper that held their parents hostage. In many cases, having money cost them far more than it afforded.

Raised on an every-other-weekend-and-shared-holidays schedule, many young people had two houses, two picket fences, two satellite dishes, *and* two sets of parents. Yet even this double-your-money American Dream could not guarantee wholesomeness.

Most young people, then, would probably not be surprised by the observations of Joseph Heath and Andrew Potter, authors of *Nation of Rebels: Why Counterculture Became Consumer Culture*, who found that after a certain point, more money does not necessarily mean more happiness. As young adults know all too well, the extra zeroes in the paycheck don't always pay off. "People are working harder, are under more stress, and are finding themselves with less free time."[26]

Many young adults, then, are abandoning workaholism to seek quality of life over quantity of dollars and possessions, a trend that was evident in a recent 2012 study from Pew Forum, which found that even though young adults were hardest hit by the recession, they emerged more content than older adults. "Among those ages 18 to 34, nearly nine-in-ten (88%) say they either have or earn enough money now or expect they will in the future. Only 9% say they don't think they will ever have enough to live the life they want. Adults ages 35 and older are much less optimistic."[27]

That said, young people aren't anti-money. They like a tall stack of presidents as much as the next generation. But while they still want to find good jobs and be paid what they're worth, they don't want the dollar signs to control them. They are conscious of the dangers that correspond with financial security and "much likelier to prioritize well-being values over survival values than old people."[28] As Chris Michalak, human resources consultant for Towers Perrin, captured it, the older generation "lives to work" while the young "work to live."[29]

5. Young people are conditioned to expect instant gratification.

Eric Chester, author of *Employing Generation Why*, observed that young people adopt a fast pace. "[Members of Generation Y] have been programmed to live life at a rapid pace to keep up with the constant change that is happening around them. They see life as a drop-down menu of choices that can be accessed immediately with the click of a mouse. Speed, change, and uncertainty are normal for Ys."[30]

Even though their surrounding culture moves quickly, young people are always trying to think of ways to make it faster. They expect things to happen so fast, in fact, that a computer science professor at UMass – Amherst who examined the viewing habits of 6.7 million Internet users in a study released in the fall of 2012 found that subjects were only willing to wait two seconds for an Internet video to load.[31]

Retailers, of course, are trying to capitalize on this generation's instant need. Walmart and Amazon, for example, have begun battling for the same-day delivery market. In Boston, which is one of the areas where Amazon same-day delivery is available, shoppers can place an order by 11:00 a.m. and, for under $10, have it arrive at their house that day. To stay competitive, Walmart launched Walmart To Go last year, charging $10 for same-day delivery, though it is not yet available everywhere.[32]

While observing culture, Dana Levin, a student at Drexel University College of Medicine, wrote, "The biggest consequence I foresee is an expectation of immediacy and decreased patience among people. Those who grow up with immediate access to media, quick response to email and rapid answers to all questions may be less likely to take longer routes to find information, seeking 'quick fixes' rather than taking the time to come to a conclusion or investigate an answer."[33]

The Pew Research Center's Internet & American Life Project reinforces these fears. Their recent study found the pace of people under the age of thirty-five had some noticeable drawbacks: "Negative effects include a need for instant gratification and loss of patience." They may become easily frustrated with problems or tasks that cannot be resolved right away.[34] Similarly, they can be famously intolerant of people who don't function as rapidly as they do.

In all the fast-paced mayhem, there are a few positive implications as well. Young people are inclined to take in information fast, process things immediately, and act on the spot to get things done. Many of them thrive in busy environments.

One way churches can harness young adults' rapid-paced energy is by calling for spontaneous involvement. For instance, rather than scheduling church "work days" for some Saturday two months from now, I've seen a huge response from young people to last-minute announcements asking, "If anyone can stay after service to help out with this, we would appreciate it." The same thing goes with social get-togethers. When I helped with twenty- and thirtysomething small groups at Westwinds Community Church in Jackson, Michigan, we often got a good turnout at preplanned social outings. However, the attendance at scheduled events never matched the outpouring of people who would join us when we hastily drew maps on the back of our bulletins for impromptu Sunday afternoon picnics or volleyball tournaments.

6. Young people like technology, but they prefer human contact.

While we're on the subject of instant gratification, let me offer a word of caution to churches trying to tune in to young people's eighty-mile-an-hour techno drive. Thanks to their rapid culture, it can be easy to assume that young adults crave a church of constantly changing flash animation and live-action video footage. But I should let you in on a secret: while young people appreciate and are familiar with multilayered technology, they are at the same time very skeptical of our complex, media-driven, advertising-crazed world.

In fact, that might be exactly the wrong strategy, since — according to one ComScore report titled *Next-Generation Strategies for Advertising to Millennials* — the battle to entertain young people is a losing one. Millennials, they found, were less interested and more difficult to connect with than previous generations. It was hard to capture their attention, impress them, or persuade them. The thing the study found young people paid the most attention to? Engaging content.[35]

Sometimes, to the contrary, young people want their God and their faith to be different from and *more real than* special effects and airbrushed images on a TV screen. They *don't* want to feel like we worship on an *American Idol* set. They *don't* want the offering spiel to come off like a host introducing the next phase of a reality TV show. And they *don't* want the morning message to rival Internet video infomercials with quick promises to improve lives overnight.

They are hungry for a real God — the ancient, timeless one who created the entire universe from chaos — and they don't think that he has to wait on the next MTV fad or Microsoft update to deliver fresh spiritual experiences.

There *is* such a thing as too much technology, as highlighted by a wave of pushback emerging from technology users writing articles like "Why Today's Hi-Tech Cars Can Drive You Crazy,"[36] "Is Your High-Tech Life Making You Sick?,"[37] and "Kids and Tech: How Much Is Too Much?"[38]

So please, church service design teams, on behalf of young people everywhere, if you have strobe lights flashing, fine. But while the sanctuary is caught up in your makeshift lightning storm, please don't also ask attendees to watch swirling words or blinking images on a screen — or all three simultaneously. Contrary to some people's beliefs, dizziness is not the new "cool" way to experience God. Technologically savvy or not, young people feel like they just got off a merry-go-round, same as you.

You know what does get their attention? Engaging, relevant content. Put real, live humans in front of them and have them talk about their real lives.

7. Young people are less relativistic than they seem.

Sometimes Christians believe young people are giving up strong positions on moral issues and becoming more wishy-washy about what they believe is right and wrong. This may be because young people tend to favor voicing their ideas in open-minded conversation with those they disagree with rather than, say, picketing an abortion clinic while waving posters of aborted fetus parts.

But on the picket lines or not, young adults' ideal world is not one where confusion runs rampant and moral imperatives are near extinction. As one of my fiftysomething friends is fond of pointing out, no matter how relativistic people may seem, if you break into their garages and steal their cars, they will declare that your worldview — which allows you to take what belongs to them — is completely and totally wrong.

Rather, I'd like to suggest that young people *do* believe in rights and wrongs. In fact, the strength of some of their opinions might surprise you. *Glamour* magazine, for instance, ran an article titled "The Mysterious Disappearance of Young Pro-Choice Women" in 2005. According to this article, eighteen- to twenty-nine-year-olds surveyed in a CBS/ *New York Times* poll were "more conservative about abortion rights than women in every other age category — except women old enough to be their grandmothers, 65 and up!"[39] *Glamour* writer Susan Dominus acknowledged, "This slow but steady seismic shift has gone mostly under the radar, but the reverberations may end up deciding the future of abortion in this country."[40]

Abortion research is often hotly debated, but today's young people seem to consistently position themselves *against* abortion more than generations before them. In 2008, for instance, a decade of Pew Research Center polls showed that eighteen- to twenty-nine-year-olds are consistently more likely than the general adult population to favor strict limits on abortion.[41] A few years later, a 2013 study by the College Republican National Committee found a growing number (51 percent) of young people lean toward prohibiting abortion. And this echoed a 2012 Harvard Institution of Politics survey of young Americans that suggested 50 percent lean toward prohibiting abortion in the vast majority of cases.[42]

8. Twentysomethings are idealistic to a fault.

If you read the description for *Delaying the Real World*, a book released in 2005, you will be greeted by the following message:

> The Cubicle Can Wait for an Adventure or Two! Congratula-
> tions — you've finished school. But if you're not sure you're
> ready to settle down into an office environment, *Delaying the
> Real World* is chock-full of creative ideas and practical informa-
> tion that will help you craft your own life-changing adventure:
>   Teach English in Thailand. Take a road trip. Build houses in
> a Mexican village. Counsel at a children's art camp. Work on a
> cruise ship. Lead excursions in the Grand Canyon. Intern at a
> wildlife sanctuary. Bike (or drive) across America. Guide snor-
> keling groups in Australia. Hike along the Pacific Trail. Create
> (and fund) your own service project. Travel around the globe on
> one affordable plane ticket. And much more![43]

It would be hard to find a better example of young people's ideal-ism than this book's author, Colleen Kinder. Kinder and her book were inspired by young adults who were graduating college but didn't want to take their place on the starting blocks of the rat race. "I started asking around and I found a lot of people were taking a year to do something that had absolutely nothing to do with their planned career."[44]

This trend of delaying adulthood, which Kinder observed in 2005, seems only to have gained momentum in the years that followed. In 2010, for instance, Frank F. Furstenberg, who leads the MacArthur Foundation Research Network on Transitions to Adulthood, observed, "People between 20 and 34 are taking longer to finish their educations, establish themselves in careers, marry, have children and become financially independent."[45] By the time 2012 arrived, in fact, a full 51 percent of eighteen- to twenty-nine-year-olds indicated they did not feel they had fully reached adulthood.[46]

When young people finally do buckle down and go to work, their idealism appears to remain intact. Dr. Randall Hansen, webmaster of Quintessential Careers (quintcareers.com), continues to see their trademark flair for idealism. "Twentysomethings around the globe struggle with the transition from college to career — and not just to career, but to the perfect career."[47] Along the way, according to the Future Workplace's report *Multiple Generations at Work*, 91 percent of millennials expect to stay in a job for less than three years, which would mean they'd hold fifteen to twenty jobs over the course of their lives![48]

It's no surprise, then, that young people tend to apply these same idealistic ideas to a search for the perfect church. When they don't find perfection, some may start to get antsy. Hence, people like Craig Dunham have begun studying how the church can retain young adults. And Dunham's findings are not especially surprising. In order for these idealistic young people to plug into churches, he says they "need the sense of real responsibility, and the authority needed to accomplish the assigned task."[49]

9. Young people value their local community.

Older generations may observe young adults being obsessed with technology that connects them with people across the world, but ironically, young people are becoming strong advocates for local community.

When the 80 million members of Generation Y settle into homes, for example, the impact on real estate and the economy will be "as striking and long-lasting as that of the baby boomers," says Leanne Lachman, Urban Land Institute (ULI) governor.[50] And research shows young people want something very specific. They want a localized life where they can walk to where they need to go. A National Association of Realtors study that surveyed 2,000 people nationwide in 2011 found that

47 percent of respondents would like to live in a downtown, an inner-city residential neighborhood, or a suburb with shops and amenities within walking distance.[51] Similar findings from RCLCO, a marketing consulting and research firm headquartered in the District of Columbia, indicated that in choosing housing, echo boomers are largely driven by proximity to work, neighborhood walkability, and price.[52] This trend, perhaps, is best captured in Donald Appleyard's book, *Livable Streets.*[53]

And they don't just want to live local. They want to shop local too. Urban Land Institute's research has shown more than half of millennials go at least once a month to discount department stores (91 percent), neighborhood shopping centers (74 percent), malls and department stores (64 percent), and chain apparel stores (58 percent), though 45 percent spend more than an hour a day looking at retail websites. According to the research, pedestrian-oriented developments appealed to Gen Y.[54]

The "buy local" movement now has official groups in 130 cities or regions, representing about thirty thousand businesses, up from forty-one cities in 2006. Lobbying points for this movement include "The 10% Shift" campaign, which rallies shoppers to shift 10 percent of their purchases to local stores, and the "Move Your Money" initiative, which asks citizens to move their money from a national bank to a local bank or credit union, claiming that smaller banks usually are more support-ive of small businesses.[55] This move to loving the local scene even has leading national corporations like Starbucks busy executing unbranding campaigns.[56]

Young people are also breathing new life and energy into the practice of community gardens. While there is still a need for national data on the increasing presence of community gardens — plots of land worked and shared by local citizens — there is ample evidence this cooperative gardening is becoming a nationwide trend as the garden-ing scene erupts in Denver,[57] Grand Rapids[58], Portland[59], Boston,[60] and other sample cities. Canada, too, seems to be experiencing a similar resurgence in gardening. Community gardens are reported to be growing at a record pace across Vancouver, for example.[61]

Young people's appreciation for local living, then, may present churches with obvious opportunity. Local congregations may be able to get their young adults more excited about being involved, for instance, by developing robust initiatives aimed at building relationships with the groups in their communities. It was surging interest in local and humanitarian efforts among the young, in fact, that led me to write my recent resource for churches, *Portable Faith: How to Take Your Church to the Community*.[62]

But young people's love of community may also find healthy expression in church small groups. During my twenties, I had the chance to be part of several young adult small groups. So many, in fact, that I have a hard time remembering exactly how many groups I've been a part of or even who attended which group.

Maybe the groups blur together because the young adults in our church never fully embraced the textbook small-group model. In fact, we broke every rule in our dust-collecting small group leader's manual. We did not stay on topic. We let people drone on about their personal issues for hours. We cried. We prayed. We held heated debates (among our favorites was an intense argument over the likelihood of flying cars). We hardly ever completed our entire discussion of the week's curriculum. And although we managed a couple of dinner outings over the course of many years, we certainly didn't fill our calendar with scheduled small-group events.

Worst of all, we never quite got the group-birthing process down smoothly. Sure, we birthed new small groups in an effort to multiply, but somehow the same people seemed to cycle in and out of all of them. No one had perfect attendance, but everyone seemed to show up at least irregularly. At least one young woman I know of even went to more than one small group so she could keep in touch with everyone.

Eventually, whether it was small-group season or not and whether we were listed in the directory or not, the young adults were hanging out so regularly that the small groups themselves kind of melted into the background.

Every Sunday we crossed paths constantly while serving as church greeters or children's ministry workers. As we passed each other, we would exchange knowing smiles and feelings of enthusiasm for the causes we were teamed in. Sometime during the morning, at least one person — often a different person each week — would take the initiative to ask, "So, are we doing anything after church today?"

The answer was almost always yes. Although we rarely did any pre-planning during the week, the young people in our church routinely set aside Sunday afternoons to hang out together.

Before you knew it, we were borrowing black Sharpies from the information table and sketching off-scale maps to our chosen meeting location on the backs of bulletins or offering envelopes or whatever else was available. After photocopying our makeshift maps into even poorer quality duplicates, we would hand them out to anyone we knew who was even remotely tied to our age group. (Our young adult group was often referred to as the twenty/thirtysomething group, but no one noticed when people on either end of the continuum stretched the age limit even past that.)

On the bottom of our maps we would inevitably scribble any other necessary information for participating in the day's events. One common addition was the reminder to bring snacks of some kind. Whatever we were doing, whether it was playing football or volleyball, watching Star Wars marathons, or playing board games, it always required food.

We never bothered to organize an official hospitality team. Instead, our meals were more like the smorgasbords a family has the night before Mom goes grocery shopping — everybody just kind of eats what they can find. And so one person might bring two chicken breasts and another a steak — yes, one steak — and yet another a pack of hot dogs. Our favorite components — potato chips with sour cream dip, tortilla chips and salsa, and Ruby Red Squirt — were so simple they wouldn't even qualify as a potluck.

But don't think young people's drive for community is centered around impromptu sporting events and food. There were plenty of real-life decisions and hassles to walk through together as well. Whether the issue was dating, illness, death, or depression, there was a seemingly endless list of situations that forced us to dig deep and learn hard spiritual truths that strengthened our relationships even further.

So we enjoy small-group community. But who doesn't? Ahh, but our expressions of community go much further than that. The building where my two best friends and I led a women's small group eventually became home to ten of us — April, Jennie, Bethany, Diane, Scott, Melanie, Amanda, Nate, Melissa, and myself — who at one time or another lived in the two upstairs apartments. In addition, over the course of a few years, seven different people with connections to our group worked at the mental health organization where I worked in college. Finally, if I'm counting correctly, this same group has attended, participated in, or helped set up/tear down at least ten church-related weddings for each other. In my wedding alone, former small-group members served as bridesmaids, band members, decorators, and even one of the pastors!

While we may have failed our small-group test, our small-group mentoring coaches hardly ever felt the need to check in with us.

And with good reason.

Young people are lovers of community.

10. Twentysomethings want to help.

Awhile back, my friend Sarah Burkel was standing in line waiting to purchase an item at a Detroit-area electronics store.

Like most people, Sarah had plenty of other things she wanted to do that day and was hoping that she would be able to quickly check out and get on with her to-do list.

No such luck.

For whatever reason, one customer's transaction was taking forever. Several minutes later, when the cashier finally closed the drawer and handed the receipt to the woman who had been ahead of Sarah, the female customer became increasingly distressed.

As Sarah waited even longer, she could overhear the dialogue as the woman — whose thick accent gave away her Eastern origin — explained that she had missed the city bus and would now have to walk home with the stereo she had just purchased.

As Sarah imagined this woman, apparently unaccustomed to life in the United States, lugging a stereo back to her home several miles away, she contemplated whether it was wise to offer the stranger a ride. Unfortunately, the woman exited the store before Sarah had a chance to come to a decision. A bit disappointed, but also relieved from having to extend herself, Sarah hopped into her car and began driving home — a drive that would have been a short trip had she not immediately passed the woman, who was trying to balance the stereo on her hip as she meandered home on foot.

Sarah pulled over to give the woman a ride, but from there her endeavor got more complicated. It turned out the woman didn't know how to get back to her home by car. She only knew the bus route. Sarah was undeterred. In following what little information they had, the two of them worked together to find their way back to the woman's apartment.

Along the way, Sarah and the woman talked about all kinds of things, from family to faith. It turned out, this woman was living in a practically empty apartment by herself as she worked to try to earn enough money to bring her husband and children to the United States to join her.

On that day, she confessed, she had been so lonely that she had finally broken down and gone to the store to purchase a CD player so her sparse apartment wouldn't always sound so quiet and lonely. What could have been a disastrous walk home immersed in even deeper loneliness became an uplifting connection, thanks to Sarah's willingness to go out of her way for a stranger who had been holding up the line in front of her.

Young people like Sarah want to help. This particular attribute, this desire to help, has been frequently noticed by experts who have studied younger generations in depth. Eric Chester, author of *Employing Generation Why*, noticed that volunteerism is at an all-time high "thanks to the unprecedented involvement of Generation Y, who are putting their time where their hearts are. It is hard to find an organized student club, sport, or activity where participants aren't involved in some type of community service as a part of their credo. Soccer teams stick around after their games to help clean up the park. Student councils visit nursing homes, paint homes for the elderly, and hold canned food drives. Cheerleaders volunteer to take underprivileged children trick or treating."[63]

A study of 4,363 young people by dosomething.org found more than half of American teenagers and young adults volunteered last year, leading the study's authors to conclude: "Young people are a secret weapon. A donation pitch from a passionate teen is way more influential than a cold call or that newsletter you were thinking about sending."[64]

11. Young people don't pledge their allegiance lightly.

While on staff at a large nondenominational church, my colleagues and I noticed the slow-to-commit trend by young people almost by accident. Despite being active in our church for a couple of years, one of our well-known young adult volunteers seemed to be purposely avoiding the church's membership process. At first, as the staff tried to determine how to proceed, some suggested that perhaps he was just trying to be anti-institutional. But the more we talked to him, the more we understood a principle that would later manifest itself in the leadership lives of several young people: this guy was not anti-establishment; he just didn't want to formally commit to membership until he was absolutely convinced that he wanted to be fully committed to the church.

And church isn't the only thing we're slow to commit to. Young people wait longer to commit to marriage than previous generations. *Bloomberg Businessweek* reported, "For men, the average age at first marriage is 28.7, while the average woman is getting married for the first time at age 26.5." That's already up from 2007 when the average age at first marriage was 27.5 years for men and 25.6 years for women, according to the report.[65]

Young adults hold off on committing to parenthood as well. "Since 1970, the average age for first childbirth for American women has gone up by four years: from 21.5 to 25.4 years old. The average age for first-time fatherhood is now 28."[66]

To the frustration of companies around the world, young people are equally slow to commit to brand-name products. That's the reason Toyota had to rebrand an entire new line, the Scion, and require their dealers to pay $25,000 in training fees to learn how to effectively sell cars to the younger generation.[67]

The church need not be offended by young adults' hesitation to commit. Everybody, from Pepsi to the Republicans to the United States Army, is trying to figure out how to get younger generations to shift their allegiance. If you have the patience to wait for us, though, you'll find that we become loyal investors in the end. As Ann Fishman, president of Generational Targeted Marketing Corporation, claims, members of Generation Y do eventually become brand loyal. However, their loyalty only comes *after* they have been allowed to discover the brands through their own devices, such as peer recommendations or self-guided investigations over the Internet.[68]

12. Twentysomethings value diversity.

Think about the status of the world when young people arrived post – civil rights movement. Though race and economic relations were still far from perfect, the United States was starting to look and feel very different. Their history books, for instance, featured Martin Luther *and* Martin Luther King Jr., George Washington *and* George Washington Carver, Andrew Jackson *and* Jesse Jackson.

Multiple ethnic and economic groups learned in the same class-rooms during the school year and swam in the same pools during the summer. They drank at the same drinking fountains and ordered kids' meals at the same restaurants. On their buses, *everyone* wanted to ride in the back because that was the seat farthest away from the driver.

In elementary school, they were glued to the TV set to watch the *Bill Cosby Show*. Bryant and Greg Gumbel delivered their sports news, Star Jones dished up social issues, and Soledad O'Brien and Ann Curry helped them follow current events. Every morning, Al Roker told them about the weather in "their neck of the woods" while every evening, Connie Chung wished them a good night. And though they may or may not have been allowed to listen to them, they were avid followers of the later bra-baring Janet Jackson and Michael Jackson, the one-gloved moonwalker, and a host of rappers and singers like Whitney Houston, Boyz II Men, Snoop Dogg, Wu Tang Clan, Beyonce, JLo, and Kanye to follow.

They got their education on multiculturalism from *Different Strokes, Facts of Life, Webster, Family Matters*, and *Sister, Sister* before they ever enrolled in high school sociology. They learned to read from Lamar Burton, picked up their first foreign languages from Maria and the other friendly neighbors on *Sesame Street*, and memorized their first science facts alongside Ms. Frizzle and her multiethnic students on the *Magic School Bus*.

As they grew older, they had crushes on *Saved by the Bell* characters Lisa Turtle and A. C. Slater and memorized the theme song to Will Smith's *Fresh Prince of Bel-Air*. They thought that MC Hammer was too legit to quit, that Ahmad Rashad had the inside stuff, and that Arsenio Hall would one day replace Letterman. They borrowed their first karate moves from Bruce Lee and Jackie Chan, toured their first colleges with Denise Huxtable and Dwayne Wayne, and explored deep space with Captain Benjamin Sisko. And Gatorade's commercials were right on: they wanted to be like Mike because Mike made them believe they could fly.

By default, young people are the most integrated generation raised in the Western world to date. Yet their appetite for integrating diverse people into their relational circles isn't limited to the Western Hemisphere. As their local culture grew more diverse, young adults' world also grew more similar. They were somehow naturalized into the global village without ever applying for citizenship. Their routines came to include regular virtual walks in other people's shoes, courtesy of now-considered-educational TV. They looked on as tanks ravaged Tiananmen Square, as the Berlin Wall crumbled, and as Patriot missiles collided with Iraqi targets. They frowned, cheered, and frowned again — often unaware they were being slowly integrated into a global culture from the comfort of their classrooms.

And the older they got, the more the world came to them. Before they knew it, they could meet, chat, email, date, and even talk about their faith with people from an expanding list of countries via the World Wide Web. If they did want to see the world firsthand, that became more doable too. Travelocity, Orbitz, Expedia, and CheapTickets.com brought intense competition to the airline industry and offered travelers discounted fares that were previously purchased only by the well-off.

For good and bad, diversity and global thinking snuck into young people's political scene too. Magic Johnson lobbied for AIDS research. Rosie and Ellen supported gay rights. Bono advocated for relief in the developing world. Superman (aka Christopher Reeve) pushed the issue of stem cell research. Brad and Angelina and Madonna championed international adoption. Affirmative action, handicap accessibility, religious postings in public buildings, and civil unions became matters for the courts to decide. Oh, and did I mention they helped elect the first African American president of the United States?

As you can see, for those raised in such a diverse and integrated society, adopting a more inclusive approach to everyday life was not just an option but — at some level — a necessity for survival.

Now, as young people wander into the arena of adults, their world is no less diverse. In fact, as of the 2010 US Census, white people no longer account for the majority of births in the United States.[69] Parents who identified their race as just "white" accounted for 49.6 percent of all births in the preceding twelve-month period, according to the Census Bureau. And minorities — Hispanics, blacks, Asians, and all those of mixed race — reached 50.4 percent, becoming the majority for the first time in the country's history.

When you count the adults and not just recently born babies, whites will remain a majority for some time, but clearly in the next few decades the ethnic makeup of the country will change. "This is an important tipping point," said William H. Frey, senior demographer at the Brookings Institution, who described the shift as a "transformation from a mostly white baby boomer culture to the more globalized multiethnic country that we are becoming."[70]

Diversity is not just a racial issue. Family arrangements are becoming more varied. In 2012, 24 percent of children lived with only their mothers, 4 percent lived with only their fathers, and 4 percent lived with neither of their parents. Sixty-four percent lived with two parents, but in 8 percent of those cases, the two parents were both a biological or adoptive parent and a stepparent. About 1.5 million lived with grandparents, 600,000 lived with nonparent relatives, and 93,000 lived with foster parents.[71]

Physically speaking, 18.7 percent of people in the United States live with some type of long-lasting condition or disability,[72] meaning that nearly one in five citizens is categorized as disabled. And linguistically, 21 percent (60.6 million) of people speak a language other than English in their homes, while 7 percent don't speak English at all.[73]

Educationally, the United States continues to be dominated by three different groups: as of 2010, almost 30 percent of adults had earned their bachelor's degree, 57 percent had earned a high school diploma or equivalency, and 13 percent had not completed high school.[74] Economically, Americans also find themselves in three primary groups: 43.2 percent of households make between $25,000 and $75,000 per year, 17.8 percent make under $25,000, and 39.1 percent make more than $75,000.[75]

To young adults nursed and immersed in such a mixed culture, it is only natural to expect churches to be intentionally inclusive of society's diverse people groups. However, they are sometimes grossly disappointed. Churches are not always perceived as welcoming — especially to groups of people unlike the majority of their attendees.

I am not surprised by the observations of author and speaker Marilyn Brenden, who writes:

> Usually the cause [behind why people leave church groups] originates from one of two things: a failure of the group to assimilate the person or personal issues in the class member's life. Unfortunately, when a class has been together for a long time, the "old" members may cluster together in an exclusive huddle. New members feel a barrier in trying to join in. As one new member put it, "They drew a circle and left me out."[76]

Take a look at the racial makeup of our local congregations, for instance. Research led by Dr. Michael Emerson, coauthor of *Divided by Faith* and *Sociology of Religion*, shows that only about 7 percent of all American congregations are multiracial. Focus solely on Protestant movements and the numbers dip even lower. Only 5 percent of Protestant congregations are multiracial.[77]

But let's not get hung up on just the race card. As Tom Huang, an editor at the *Dallas Morning News*, points out, young people's subcultures — such as hip-hop, skateboarding, anime, video games, and extreme sports — are "beginning to transcend race."[78]

Likewise, there are other groups — outside of racial ones — that should be on the church's radar too. While completing my urban studies minor, I made lists of other people groups who were seemingly missing in action from the white, middle-class churches I attended growing up. These people included, but were not limited to, addicts, adult entertainment employees, AIDS victims, blue-collar workers, divorcees, those suffering from eating disorders, the elderly, foster care children, gangs,

Goths, the homebound, the homeless, homosexuals, the hospitalized, the illiterate, immigrants, low-income families, the mentally ill, minority races, the non – English speaking, the physically challenged, pregnant teens, prisoners, those dependent on public transportation, runaways, the socially challenged, single parents, skaters, unwed mothers, the undereducated, the unemployed, vegans, the visually impaired, those dependent on welfare, and widows and widowers.

Let me give you an example of one of the statements I made early on that raised many an "okay, that might be true, but you still shouldn't have said it" eyebrow. I have often noted that I could go to an Eminem concert and put my hands in the air ("Everybody in the 313, put your hands up and follow me") alongside every socioeconomic and racial group in the United States. Yet if I go to church the next day, I point out, I'd be raising my hands with a thousand other people of the same race and general social class.

Do I say this because I like to incite controversy? Um, well, maybe just a little. But do I say this because I'm political? Because I'm a relativist? Because I have a penchant for swaying to cheesy songs? No. The real question is not "How can we get the church to be more like an Eminem concert?" (which, by the way, doesn't have as wide of an age sampling despite its economic and racial diversity). The more important question is "What does the lack of diversity in many churches show us about the condition of our hearts and the effectiveness of our collective mission?"

The church's ability to engage its diverse world is not a political issue; it is a missional issue. An obedience issue. A "do you take Jesus' parting shot to his disciples seriously?" issue. The heart of the matter is not *racial* or *economic* reconciliation, but *spiritual* reconciliation.

Just as "giving our lives to Christ" involves shifting our allegiance each day we wake up, one day at a time, "going into all the world" involves being the church to each person we encounter, one person at a time. Eventually, if we make it through enough people, we are — by default — destined to run into some people unlike ourselves. The road to reaching the world, then, runs straight through the middle of diverse people groups.

Appendix C:
Resources for
Denominational Leaders

TEN IDEAS FOR FIGHTING DISILLUSIONMENT AT A DENOMINATIONAL LEVEL

1. Put together a feedback session or retreat for young attendees or leaders across the denomination to come and offer feedback about the future of your organization.
2. Purposefully recruit or promote qualified young people to join your executive staff or planning committees so you will always have a representative voice as you shape new initiatives and programming.
3. Ensure your denomination or network is actively engaging people on social networks as well as keeping your website up to date, since these are places young people may seek spiritual information. Similarly, if you haven't already, try to get your sermons recorded in a format that can be archived and kept available online.
4. Create opportunities for young pastors and church staff to find veteran mentors and create communication channels for them to use to find support when they are in trouble.
5. Offer ongoing opportunities for training for younger people, and if needed, provide scholarships for the youngest members

heading up small churches who might not have the financial resources to attend.

6. Listen, survey, and intentionally collect data in an attempt to understand young people's points of view, and look for ideas that may encourage them to engage the things God lays on their hearts. For example, could the denomination endorse a new kind of ministry that engages young people and then encourage local congregations to adopt this ministry to give their young people a chance to be involved in something they especially care about?

7. Develop and train churches to follow a robust plan, including age-relevant curriculum, for creating a strong, intentional transition between high school youth group and adult ministries across your denomination.

8. Help pastors learn to recognize and respond to disillusionment in their own congregation members, including helping them develop good skills and systems to follow up with church attendees who leave their local settings.

9. Help churches find out what young people are doing in their communities, and encourage them to offer those services for free or at low cost in your church building. Create free fitness classes, for example.

10. Encourage churches to go where young people are. If they attend book clubs, go to meet-ups, join sports leagues, and get out in their communities, they are more likely to build relationships with young adults. And the more of your church people who are in relationship with young adults, the more likely young adults are to develop some kind of relationship with a local church and the denomination.

Appendix D:
Resources for Parents and Family Members of the Disillusioned

Dear Parents and other concerned family members,

While working with high school students and young adults for more than a decade, in both the church and public school system, I often encountered parents who were exasperated with their children as the kids grew toward adulthood. Their children's behaviors — poor social choices, resistance to traditional values, and attitudes toward faith, for example — often left parents consumed with worry about a child's adult development.

Many times parents' emotions would spiral and they would fear the worst. Would their kids soon abandon all they knew and live a reckless life that brought them ongoing cycles of trouble? Was all of the energy invested in their child's faith and wholesomeness wasted? Would their child have any connection to God or the community of faith they were raised in?

Certainly every case is different. And there are kids who get stuck in cycles of hardship that stay with them for many years and even decades. But that was usually not the norm I observed. Instead, while watching class after class of young people grow up and graduate and move through their young adult years, I often noticed they often emerged as remarkably balanced people compared to their troubled teenage selves. Sometimes, in fact, I would be blown away by the mammoth difference between a child's freshman year of high school — marked by apathy and general squirreliness and disorder — and their sophomore year, where they were suddenly rooted and highly capable of managing the responsibilities life thrust upon them. Twelve months sometimes produced students I barely recognized.

In these cases, I occasionally had the pleasure of retaining contact with parents who were of course incredibly relieved that their children seemed to be considerably healthier than they had feared. I would regularly ask these parents, in these celebratory instances, what they thought the difference maker was for their child. And I can't tell you how many times they shrugged and said something like, "I guess it was just time. It seems like he just needed time to settle in and figure out what he believed and find his own way."

I found something simply and profoundly true in their observations. Often what people in their teens and twenties (and even older) need most is time and space to find (or refind) their way. They may need to explore a little bit, and they may venture outside the bounds of what they've known, but many of the ones I observed eventually reestablished and recentered themselves in a stabler place that they chose for themselves. I have seen this happen more times than I can count.

The good that you, as a parent or loved one, instilled in them and the positives they experienced in faith community are still in them. They encounter spiritual references and ideas in their movies, songs, television shows, and conversations. They wrestle with matters of God and faith and what this world means as they fall asleep at night. Everything they've heard and seen is stored inside them still to this day. There is something to be said for giving them time.

But what to do in the meantime, while your son's or daughter's or other relative's actions seem to threaten their well-being and sense of stability or seem to infringe on their relationship with God and church? There are no magic or instant answers that will bring about immediate change or recovery. The best I have is simply this: *While you're giving them time to grow, give them your time as well.*

Express that you love them, be willing to listen nonjudgmentally and for long periods of time, respect their right to find their way, and speak positively about their future. Indicate that you want them around no matter what. Keeping a healthy, open relationship increases the likelihood that you'll be able to continue to invest in them as they find their way.

And in the moments that seem particularly challenging, I offer you this small bit of comfort I've taken more than a few times in life. Even on our worst days, in cycles of bad decisions, God never loses track of where we are. He never loses your child's file or forgets his or her name. And nothing on earth — nothing your child does, nothing your child's friends or lovers or influencers do — can separate them from the love of God.

I hope you will take hope, dear parents, and stay the course.

Sarah

TIPS FOR BEING SUPPORTIVE WITHOUT OVERSTEPPING YOUR CHILDREN'S NEED TO EXPLORE AND OWN THEIR FAITH FOR THEMSELVES

Allow God to be mysterious sometimes. Rather than trying to thrust hand-selected information about God on children or other mentees, I am learning to acknowledge that what we are inviting others into is an interactive mystery — some of which we can't fully explain and shouldn't try to, some of which is yet to be fully understood. I have found that faith is owned and internalized at a far more intense rate when we allow people to explore genuinely, to seek truth, and not just keep repeating or protecting our preselected answers.

Define faith beyond just a simple repeat-after-me prayer or adoption of the label "Christian." Sometimes the disillusioned resist the idea of a formal conversion or they distance themselves from denominational or Christian vocabulary and affiliations because they are uncomfortable with something about the way religion is sometimes mechanized or presented in a way that strikes them as insincere. In my experience, many times this reactiveness — this attempt to disconnect with what they deem false impressions of faith — is a positive that suggests they believe there is a *better* or *more authentic* way of knowing God and seeking and living truth. In many cases I've observed, disillusioned people often experience a paradigm shift in which they begin to see church as something bigger than a building, something they want to *live* and *be*, not just a place they want to attend once a week. Often this is a move toward deeper, more honest faith than simply going through the religious motions. There's a good chance, too, that as the disillusioned work through their frustrations and find new ways to express their belief in God, they will return to church communities or replace them with similar affiliations that offer rhythms of worship, biblical learning, and community.

Accept that even when people choose a different path than you would choose for them, they are exercising their God-given right to do so. Rather than panicking or excessively interfering with their choices, be assured that God can reveal himself just as well through any painful consequences they experience as he can in the church. Mistakes are not necessarily dead ends; often they are expressways to enlightenment. In releasing some of the control factor to God, you will be demonstrating that you *authentically* believe that God is capable of revealing himself and transforming lives without you overseeing every step of the process.

Realize that our best witness is often our most natural one. Many of us want to overprepare ourselves so we can articulately and convincingly explain the salvation plan to others. We want to feel intellectually strong enough to outdebate and outwit any person who is resistant to the faith. We want to fight skepticism and cynicism with knowledge and facts. But in my experience, this rehearsed style of evangelism often seems to run contrary to what actually draws people to God. Most people in my life are only marginally influenced by my memorized salvation verbiage. Quite the opposite, I am able to communicate the reality of God best based on whether or not God is reflected in my reality. Our best evangelism involves beliefs, yes, but most people (at least Americans) are aware of the basic tenets of Christianity, so it is not information they are lacking. What makes the difference, what breathes life into those beliefs and turns information into transformation, is often prolonged life-on-life contact.

Take advantage of natural, routine opportunities to disciple others, rather than investing a disproportionate amount of time and energy into church-orchestrated programs. We often forget that Jesus' idea of spreading faith was not based on blueprints or diagrams of a church hierarchy, but rather a choice to invest in twelve people. Churches often do a great job of encouraging us to serve in ministry areas that benefit those already coming to church, but sometimes it is good for us — as people who love the disillusioned — to practice living our faith outside the hour or few hours each week we are in church. Engaging the broader community, say, via a book group or exercise class will help you interact with locals, learn about how the broader unchurched culture thinks about religion and spirituality, and perhaps give you good opportunity to interact with the disillusioned people you love outside of the church they are currently not attending.

Disciple others broadly so that they are not just equipped to serve in your specific church's programs but can recognize and respond to God's movement in their lives no matter what the context. Often, as church leaders or as parents, we have a personal preference that our children grow up and experience faith the same way we do. We'd love it if they stuck with our denomination or even continued attending our church and sitting in our family pew for the rest of their lives. And this is an understandable desire often based in love and a healthy desire to remain connected. But it is wise to approach discipleship more open-handedly, hoping to inspire our children or loved ones to explore faith and develop disciplines that help them seek and follow God wherever they are, rather than seeing attendance at our church as the highest form of "success." That way, no matter what — whether they attend our church, change churches, or stop going to church altogether; whether they live in our town or across the planet — our children and those we disciple will know how to nurture spiritual support and accountability systems.

Invite people into a network of spiritual friendships rather than just an organization (although an organization *can* facilitate a network of spiritual friendships, this is not always the case). A person can easily miss the point of a sixty-minute service, but it is much more difficult to miss the sense of "kingdom here" that is experienced when surrounded by a group of like-minded Christ followers who are living out God's ideals in close proximity to each other. If your children or those you love are distancing themselves from formal expressions of church, try to keep them included in gatherings of friends where they will continue to interact with and observe those who are practicing the Christian faith. Remember, even if they are not in the church building on Sunday, that doesn't mean they are not interacting with people (from your church or elsewhere) who are living and being church to them fairly regularly.

Admit shortcomings more quickly and more often. Of all the people who have shared disillusioning church experiences with me, the great majority were disillusioned because someone who claimed to represent God failed to represent God's ideals in a particular situation. While part of the solution is, of course, to represent God *better*, an equally crucial part is being willing to acknowledge when our own behavior strays from our intentions.

While teaching my high school students, I took up a new practice: following my apologies with one simple statement, "That is not who I want to be." If I speak too harshly or hastily to a student, I immediately try to retrace my steps. "I'm sorry for being short with you. That is not who I want to be." By doing this, I believe I reinforce what type of behavior belongs in a healthy Christian life and I am admitting that certain behaviors have no place in one. This practice with my students has single-handedly increased my credibility beyond anything else I have ever done.

Forgive more quickly and more often. When church people judge others too harshly, we create a climate of spiritual perfectionism in which people are afraid to be honest about barriers to their own spiritual growth. I have found that forgiveness — like salvation — must extend past a simple exchange of words. Forgiveness is an attitude that implies an internal understanding that we are no better than anyone else around us. Forgiveness infers that we will not only verbally forgive, but also create space for others to forge their own faith where we don't hold their failures against them.

Define salvation as the Bible does — as "belief." Oftentimes we want those we love to experience faith as we do. We hope they'll enjoy the same pattern and rhythm of church attendance, volunteer involvement, devotional time, and so on. But these expectations, though well-intentioned, can often come off as pressure. Focus on what the Bible says about following Christ. It is *belief* that makes someone a disciple (John 8:31), *belief* that deems them God's children (John 1:12), and *belief* that qualifies them as children of Abraham (Galatians 3:7). *Belief* is also the qualifier that allowed tax collectors and prostitutes to enter the kingdom's door ahead of the religious leaders who questioned Jesus' divinity (Matthew 21:31 – 32).

Throughout the New Testament, we see this same mode of entry revisited by author after author. Paul reminded people that the Spirit doesn't move because you observe the law but because you *believe* what you've heard (Galatians 3:5). Peter taught that it was only through *belief* in God that people had hope (1 Peter 1:21). John passed on a similarly simple command: *believe* in the name of God's Son, Jesus Christ, and love one another as he commanded us (1 John 3:23). Even the chief priests and Pharisees feared that if Jesus continued to do miracles, more people would *believe* (John 11:48). In fact, belief was apparently such a central part of Christians' identities that they were referred to as *believers* (Acts 4:32 is just one example).

Interestingly enough, from Nicodemus (John 3) to Zacchaeus (Luke 19), the Samaritan townspeople (John 4:39 – 42) to the disciples (Matthew 4, Mark 3, Luke 5, John 1), not one person is asked to sign a list of doctrines.

In fact, there is no "repeat after me." No "raise a hand." No "ask Jesus into your heart."

Just believe.

If your children believe but their belief manifests differently than yours, give them space.

THE IMPORTANCE OF AUTHENTICITY

Like it or not, it is hard to deny that the nation's drive for "authenticity" hasn't changed in the last thirty years. I was born in 1978 — the same year that First Lady Betty Ford wrote a public statement announcing she was checking into the Long Beach Naval Hospital's rehab center after overmedicating herself. At the time, not everyone thought it was appropriate for the First Lady to expose her flaws to the nation. As White House reporter Helen Thomas put it, "To be honest about an addiction problem took a lot of courage. People do not want to be considered any other way than perfect, especially first ladies."[79]

Mrs. Ford also was among the first of America's elite to talk about breast cancer and premarital sex with the cameras rolling. And not only did she broach these touchy subjects, but she occasionally offered different views than her husband's (which prompted controversy over the appropriate role of the First Lady). I guess it's easy to see why Robert Barrett, an aide to President Ford, told the *New York Times* in 1978: "We've never had too much success in keeping Mrs. Ford's mouth shut."[80]

In the eighteen years that followed Mrs. Ford's admission to Long Beach Naval Hospital, the world grew increasingly comfortable with authenticity. By the time I was old enough to vote in 1996, I could browse a 445-page online report about the extramarital affair of incumbent candidate President William Jefferson Clinton.

Even then, I never realized how raw the world had become. Not until I read this newsflash: "After Clinton's report was posted on the House of Representatives website, visitors started streaming in to the tune of three million hits per hour (66,000 hits per hour was normal)."[81] The online report was so popular, it prompted Jay Leno to quip, "I'll bet Clinton's glad he put a computer in every classroom."[82]

President Clinton's intern mishaps were not the only executive branch blunders that made public airwaves. Comedians from David Letterman to the cast of *Saturday Night Live* found easy targets in everything from Vice President Dan Quayle's spelling (in)ability to President George W. Bush's speaking slipups. Although people had probably long noticed the inadequacies of politicians, the world we grew up in was willing to make fun of their flaws out loud.

Of course, in the young adults' school days, you didn't have to be a politician to have your private life broadcast for the nation. Thanks to a wide range of talk-show hosts, including Phil Donahue, Jenny Jones, Geraldo Rivera, Oprah Winfrey, Ricki Lake, and Montel Williams, viewers could look on as "average" citizens grappled with all sorts of real-life issues, from reuniting with lost relatives to confronting unfaithful lovers. "By the summer of 1993 the television page of *USA Today* listed seventeen talk shows and local papers as many as twenty-seven."[83]

Perhaps one of the rawest talk-show stories hails from Springerland. The host? Jerry Springer, a Cincinnati city councilman, who resigned in 1971 after police discovered a check he had written to a prostitute. After waiting only one year, Springer ran for city council again and was reelected. Two years later, Springer became mayor of Cincinnati at age thirty-three. After an unsuccessful attempt at winning the Ohio governorship, Springer was hired as a political reporter for NBC's Cincinnati affiliate and within two years was their Emmy-winning top news anchor. This success likely led to his talk show, *The Jerry Springer Show*, which first aired in 1991 and would proceed to gain him a reputation as the nation's smuttiest talk-show host.[84]

Perhaps it was talk shows like Springer's that led to the authenticity generation's recent phenomenon — reality TV. Just when the world thought TV couldn't get any more transparent, surveillance crews began tailing people and providing fly-on-the-wall views into everyday human routines.

In March 1989, *COPS* debuted. The plot? There really wasn't one. Cameras followed on-duty police officers as they responded to speeding violations and domestic violence disputes. Soon after came MTV's *The Real World*, which became one of the most popular and long-lasting reality shows to date. In 2002 *Big Brother* premiered in Europe and *Survivor* hit the United States. From there, reality television exploded.

The Real World, to expand on one example, topped expressions of authenticity by inserting seven young people in a New York City loft and rolling the cameras as they locked lips, slammed doors, and broke down in tears. In thirteen episodes, Andre, Becky, Eric, Heather, Julie, Kevin, and Norman launched a trend that would continue for sixteen seasons of volatile disagreements, steamy makeout sessions, and drunken escapades.

Today, as I write this, you can find a list of 530 US-based reality shows, along with 11 Canadian-based, 5 Australian-based, and 36 UK-based programs, at www.realitytvlinks.com.

Is it any surprise that a world exposed to this level of everyday drama expects its church to feel real and maybe sometimes a little bit raw as well?

If we want to engage younger generations about their disillusionment about faith, we have to prepare for some of the most honest conversations we've ever had about belief systems, church, and the Bible.

Going into a conversation, I would suggest doing the following:

Initially, just determine to listen. In the first conversation, set listening well as your only goal.

Try to walk away with a few key points. As you're talking, try to summarize or get the person you are speaking with to summarize their main concerns about church attendance or faith practices. Ask questions such as, "So would you say that hypocrisy in church leaders is the thing that bothers you most?"

Express understanding, validation, and sorrow for bad experiences wherever possible.

Try to create a safe, pressure-free environment where ideas can be explored.

Acknowledge that the disillusioned person may need time to heal and sort things out.

Rather than expressing frustration about lack of church attendance or neglect of faith practices, express encouragement about the positives those things have brought to your life.

Intentionally express how you love the disillusioned person and will provide support. Let him know that you respect that he must forge his own path.

Suggest that even if the disillusioned person feels cynical about the idea of corporate religion or organized worship, he might have something to gain just by being around people who love him.

Appendix E:
Fifty Things I've Learned about Forgiveness

1. Learn to apologize even if it seems risky or unnecessary; it is usually neither.

2. Apologizing for what you have done wrong does not mean that the person you are apologizing to bears no guilt. It just means you forgive her whether she ever understands or regrets what she has done or not.

3. If you can't apologize, it is sometimes just as beneficial to simply acknowledge someone's pain.

4. Don't ever deny someone the luxury of being human or broken. That is not a luxury you yourself can afford to lose.

5. Don't ever forget that given and received grace is the very premise of our salvation. Without it, none of us would be whole enough to forgive anyone in the first place.

6. On a secular pop-psychology level, you have a "right" to a lot of anger and hard-core bitterness. But then again, what does pop psychology *really* know compared to God?

7. When you tell people they need to repent, they often don't understand the real benefit of restoring themselves to you. Before you air their mistakes, make sure that they understand how deeply you value their relationship and how desperately

you want to maintain it. People most often respond with humility when someone casts a vision that offers them the benefits of true grace.

8. Don't relentlessly demand an apology from people who cannot see the error of their ways. Instead, trust that God's Spirit can travel into the inner recesses of their hearts where you yourself cannot go.

9. Don't purposefully numb yourself to those who have hurt you to protect yourself from further relational tension or loss. Putting up walls never creates more connectedness, and detaching yourself never repairs the distance between you and others.

10. Realize that total restoration may not come all at once. If it is to come sincerely, it may need to unfold in stages. Be patient.

11. Do *what you can* to pursue unity *as you can*. If you wait until tomorrow, things may have spiraled too far out of control to ever go back.

12. Only God knows the motives of a person's heart. Don't pretend you do.

13. Always value humans most. Saving a relationship with a person is much more important than adding another accomplishment to your résumé.

14. Live generously. Make routine "deposits" in the lives of those you are teamed with so that if you ever have to make a "withdrawal," you will have something to withdraw.

15. Don't store up your frustration. You will be tempted to let it out when it is not appropriate or helpful to do so.

16. Speaking poorly of others is like training yourself to think the worst of them. Soon you will find that they are monsters — not because they have no actual strengths, but because you have conditioned yourself not to see them.

17. Speak the truth in the small things. It will make engaging the big things so much easier.

18. Don't ever write off a relationship as too far gone. Our God is a God who helps us transcend the impossible.

19. Don't tie your ability to move on to any particular pace or outcome. Rather, commit to investing in restoration over the long haul.

20. Anytime you get the chance, speak words of restoration and grace, and encourage others to speak them too. In doing so, you create a culture that reflects Christ well.

21. Do what you need to do even when the other person isn't planning on doing his part. You wouldn't want to sacrifice your ability to live in God's blessing just to spite him, would you?

22. Avoid secret grudges, manipulative conversations, or wishy-washy go-betweening. Do everything you can whenever you can to live openhearted before all parties involved.

23. Acknowledge your own failures in trying to bring about restoration. Admit when your approach has been or is imperfect, and communicate that you are trying and want to try even harder.

24. Guard your emotions, especially when you are in leadership. People who follow you in the light will often also follow you into the darkness. Do not be responsible for taking them there.

25. Tell people what you have learned about how you could have conducted yourself better in the past. By sharing your own failings, you encourage others that it is safe for them to acknowledge their flaws as well.

26. Realize that often far more is at stake than whether you are deemed right in the end or whether the other party ever speaks the exact confession you've written out for her in your head. Other people learn what forgiveness is by how you act. Thus, the kingdom will be well served if you err on the side of generous, rather than stingy, expressions of forgiveness.

27. Do what you know is right so that you can live with a clean conscience. Do not reserve your apology for the moment when

the other party is also ready to apologize. Why should you take bitterness to the grave just because your offender never chooses to be humble?

28. Love those you are teamed with more than you love your own pride. If you don't, then what you are offering is not really love at all.

29. How long should you wait for the other party to desire restoration? As long as it takes. If you truly love that person, you will live your whole life ready to usher in greater unity at a moment's notice — no matter how long that moment takes to arrive.

30. Stick by your "do the will of our Father" family just as fiercely as you stick by your genetic family. Which do you think is stronger: our spiritual bond or our human one?

31. You will rarely find stronger love than the kind that results when someone knows your flaws and vice versa, but you choose to love each other anyway.

32. If forgiveness or restoration is not instantly achievable, then let it be known that you will be there in the mess and you will be there when the mess resolves — all the while hoping that one day things will get better.

33. Don't be quick to disassociate from others because of their flaws or their inability to acknowledge them. Our God is not quick to disassociate from us.

34. Realize that our own flaws and pain often impair our ability to see. Our lack of objectivity often makes others' motives seem far more calculated than actually is the case.

35. Because of our own bias, other people's mistakes are often far more obvious — and seemingly far more amplified — than our own. Know that your mistakes look the same way to them.

36. Don't say you have done everything you possibly can to achieve unity if you have never actually addressed a problem directly to someone's face.

37. Get all parties involved in a conflict at a table and talk things out before everyone has time to become cemented in their individual status as victims.

38. Remember that Jesus told the disciples that those who acted in his name could not easily deny him the next moment. Start by feeling unified in God's mission, and work your way up from there.

39. Remember that offering forgiveness is as much an act of furthering the kingdom as any other task on your to-do list.

40. Even if you do not speak your grudge, it is what is inside your cup that makes you unclean. Don't kid yourself by telling other people you don't have a grudge. It leaks out of you when you are not even aware you are dripping.

41. If whoever wants to be first must be last, it makes sense to sometimes be willing to go to the end of the line.

42. If you are only willing to forgive when people do exactly *what* you think they should do *when* you think they should do it, then what you are offering is not grace at all but another chance for others to applaud you for being the one who was right all along.

43. The way we go about being right is as important as being right. Sometimes the way we go about being right destroys the value of being right.

44. Don't split the church over your own personal preference. Do you really think God will think the loss to the kingdom was well worth what you sacrificed trying to be right?

45. Remember that when you fail to live in unity with those who are in God's church, your children will take note of your decision. How do you want your children to remember you?

46. Sometimes in our anger we miss opportunities to express love and support when people have failed and need that love and support the most. We would be well served to backtrack and offer the grace that we forgot to give on so many occasions.

47. Often the best way to progress in the future is to make peace with your past so it cannot travel with you to tomorrow.

48. The reality behind truth claimed to be spoken in love is that it was often not spoken in love at all.

49. When we keep a record of people's wrongs, we're more likely to look for their wrongs in the future.

50. At the end of your life, you will never wish you had read one more book or completed one more task from your inbox. But you will certainly wish that you had one more day to love someone more deeply.

Appendix F:
Resources for Learning More about Disillusionment

BOOKS

I've compiled a list of books and websites that deal with disillusionment and related experiences and have made an effort to include a variety of voices, including those who may disagree with my own perspective.

Frustration with Church

Bad Religion: How We Became a Nation of Heretics by Ross Douthat (Free Press, 2012)

Church: Why Bother? by Philip Yancey (Zondervan, 2001)

Disappointment with God by Philip Yancey (Zondervan, 1992)

Exiles: Living Missionally in a Post-Christian Culture by Michael Frost (Baker, 2006)

God without Religion: Can It Really Be This Simple? by Andrew Farley (Baker, 2011)

Healing Your Church Hurt: What to Do When You Still Love God but Have Been Wounded by His People by Stephen Mansfield and George Barna (Tyndale Momentum, 2012)

I Quit: Stop Pretending Everything Is Fine and Change Your Life by Geri Scazzero and Peter Scazzero (Zondervan, 2010)

Leaving Church: A Memoir of Faith by Barbara Brown Taylor (HarperOne, 2006)

Life after Church: God's Call to Disillusioned Christians by Brian Sanders (IVP, 2007)

Life Together: The Classic Exploration of Faith in Community by Dietrich Bonhoeffer (HarperOne, 1978)

Messy Spirituality by Michael Yaconelli (Zondervan, 2007)

The Post-Church Christian: Dealing with the Generational Baggage of Our Faith by J. Paul Nyquist and Carson Nyquist (Moody, 2013)

Quitting Church: Why the Faithful Are Fleeing and What to Do about It by Julia Duin (Baker, 2009)

So You Don't Want to Go to Church Anymore by Wayne Jacobsen and Dave Coleman (Windblown Media, 2006)

Soul Repair: Rebuilding Your Spiritual Life by Jeff VanVonderen, Dale Ryan, and Juanita Ryan (IVP, 2008)

Spiritual Abuse Recovery: Dynamic Research on Finding a Place of Wholeness by Barbara M. Orlowski (Wipf and Stock, 2010)

Still: Notes on a Mid-Faith Crisis by Lauren Winner (HarperOne, 2012)

Stop Dating the Church: Fall in Love with the Family of God by Joshua Harris (Multnomah, 2004)

Toxic Faith by Stephen Arterburn and Jack Felton (Shaw, 2001)

Why Church Matters: Discovering Your Place in the Family of God by Joshua Harris (Multnomah, 2011)

Young Adults

Essential Church: Reclaiming a Generation of Dropouts by Thom S. Rainer (B&H, 2008)

Generation Ex-Christian: Why Young Adults Are Leaving the Faith … and How to Bring Them Back by Drew Dyck (Moody, 2010)

The Juvenilization of American Christianity by Thomas Bergler (Eerdmans, 2012)

Lost and Found: The Younger Unchurched and the Churches Who Reach Them by Ed Stetzer (B&H, 2009)

The Millennials: Connecting to America's Largest Generation by Thom S. Rainer and Jess Rainer (B&H, 2011)

They Like Jesus but Not the Church by Dan Kimball (Zondervan, 2007)

Tribal Church: Ministering to the Missing Generation by Carol Howard Merritt (Alban Institute, 2007)

unChristian: What a New Generation Really Thinks about Christianity and Why It Matters by David Kinnaman and Gabe Lyons (Baker, 2012)

Why Men Hate Going to Church by David Murrow (Thomas Nelson, 2011)

You Lost Me: Why Young Christians Are Leaving Church … and Rethinking Faith by David Kinnaman (Baker, 2011)

The State of the Church

The American Church in Crisis: Groundbreaking Research Based on a National Database of Over 200,000 Churches by David T. Olson (Zondervan, 2008)

Bring 'Em Back Alive: A Healing Plan for Those Wounded by the Church by Dave Burchett (WaterBrook, 2004)

The Church in an Age of Crisis: 25 New Realities Facing Christianity by James Emery White (Baker, 2012)

Futurecast: What Today's Trends Mean for Tomorrow's World by George Barna (BarnaBooks, 2011)

The Great Evangelical Recession: 6 Factors That Will Crash the American Church … and How to Prepare by John S. Dickerson (Baker, 2013)

ReChurch: Healing Your Way Back to the People of God by Stephen Mansfield (BarnaBooks, 2010)

Revolution by George Barna (Tyndale House, 2006)

The Unchurched

Deep and Wide: Creating Churches Unchurched People Love to Attend by Andy Stanley (Zondervan, 2012)

Jim and Casper Go to Church: Frank Conversation about Faith,

Churches, and Well-Meaning Christians by Jim Henderson, Matt Casper, and George Barna (BarnaBooks, 2007)

The Outsider Interviews: A New Generation Speaks Out on Christianity by Jim Henderson, Todd Hunter, and Craig Spinks (Baker, 2010)

Surprising Insights from the Unchurched and Proven Ways to Reach Them by Thom S. Rainer (Zondervan, 2008)

The Unchurched Next Door: Understanding Faith Stages as Keys to Sharing Your Faith by Thom S. Rainer (Zondervan, 2008)

Recovery

Comeback Churches: How 300 Churches Turned Around and Yours Can Too by Ed Stetzer and Mike Dodson (B&H, 2007)

Creating a Prodigal-Friendly Church by Jeff Lucas (Zondervan, 2008)

Cure for the Common Church: God's Plan to Restore Church Health by Bob Whitesel (Wesleyan Publishing House, 2012)

Dead Church Walking: Giving Life to the Church That Is Dying to Survive by Jimmy Dorrell (IVP, 2012)

The Grace of Everyday Saints: How a Band of Believers Lost Their Church and Found Their Faith by Julian Guthrie (Houghton Mifflin Harcourt, 2011)

The U-Turn Church: New Direction for Health and Growth by Kevin G. Harney and Bob Bouwer (Baker, 2012)

When Bad Christians Happen to Good People: Where We Have Failed Each Other and How to Reverse the Damage (WaterBrook, 2011)

Who Stole My Church? What to Do When the Church You Love Tries to Enter the 21st Century by Gordon McDonald (Thomas Nelson, 2010)

Suffering/Hardship

Broken Open: How Difficult Times Can Help Us Grow by Elizabeth Lesser (Villard, 2005)

Disappointment with God by Philip Yancey (Zondervan, 1992)

A Force of Will by Mike Stavlund (Baker, 2013)

Glorious Ruin: How Suffering Sets You Free by Tullian Tchividjian (David C. Cook, 2012)

The God I Don't Understand: Reflections on Tough Questions of Faith by Christopher J. H. Wright (Zondervan, 2008)

The God Who Sees You: Look to Him When You Feel Discouraged, Forgotten, or Invisible (David C. Cook, 2012)

The Gospel according to Job: An Honest Look at Pain and Doubt from the Life of One Who Lost Everything by Mike Mason (Crossway, 1994)

A Grief Observed by C. S. Lewis (HarperOne, 2001)

Hidden Smile of God: The Fruit of Affliction in the Lives of John Bunyan, William Cowper, and David Brainerd by John Piper (Crossway, 2008)

Holding On to Hope: A Pathway through Suffering to the Heart of God by Nancy Guthrie (Tyndale Momentum, 2006)

How Can a Good God Let Bad Things Happen? by Mark A. Tabb (NavPress, 2008)

If God Is Good: Faith in the Midst of Suffering and Evil by Randy Alcorn (Multnomah, 2009)

Man's Search for Meaning by Victor Frankl (Beacon, 2006)

Night by Elie Wiesel (Hill and Wang, 2006)

The Problem of Pain by C. S. Lewis (HarperOne, 2009)

The Promise of Despair: The Way of the Cross as the Way of the Church by Andrew Root (Abingdon, 2010)

Sifted: Pursuing Growth through Trials, Challenges, and Disappointments by Wayne Cordeiro (Zondervan, 2012)

Suffering and the Sovereignty of God by John Piper and Justin Taylor (Crossway, 2006)

Surprised by Suffering: The Role of Pain and Death in the Christian Life by R. C. Sproul (Reformation Trust Publishing, 2009)

Trusting God: Even When Life Hurts by Jerry Bridges (NavPress, 2008)

Unglued: Making Wise Choices in the Midst of Raw Emotions by Lysa TerKeurst (Zondervan, 2012)

The Well-Balanced World Changer: A Field Guide for Staying Sane While Doing Good (Moody, 2013)

When Bad Things Happen to Good People by Harold S. Kushner (Anchor, 2004)

When the Darkness Will Not Lift by John Piper (Crossway, 2006)

Where Is God When It Hurts? by Philip Yancey (Zondervan, 2002)

Your Scars Are Beautiful to God: Finding Peace and Purpose in the Hurts of Your Past by Sharon Jaynes (Harvest House, 2006)

Change

Change Agent: Engaging Your Passion to Be One Who Makes a Difference by Os Hillman (Charisma House, 2011)

Change Your Church for Good by Brad Powell (Thomas Nelson, 2010)

Immunity to Change: How to Overcome It and Unlock the Potential in Yourself and Your Organization by Robert Kegan and Lisa Laskow Lahey (Harvard Business Review Press, 2009)

Leading Change by John P. Kotter (Harvard Business Review Press, 2012)

Picking Dandelions: A Search for Eden among Life's Weeds by Sarah Cunningham (Zondervan, 2010)

Preparing for Change Reaction: How to Introduce Change in Your Church by Bob Whitesel (Wesleyan Publishing House, 2008)

Remembering the Future: The Church and Change by Robert Schnase (Abingdon, 2012)

Revise Us Again: Living from a Renewed Christian Script by Frank Viola (David C. Cook, 2011)

Staying Power: Why People Leave the Church Over Change (And What You Can Do about It!) by Bob Whitesel (Abingdon, 2003)

Steering Through Chaos: Mapping a Clear Direction for Your Church in the Midst of Transition and Change by Scott Wilson (Zondervan, 2010)

Transitions: Leading Churches through Change by David N. Mosser and Robert Schnase (Westminster John Knox, 2011)

Burnout

Accidental Pharisees: Avoiding Pride, Exclusivity, and the Other Dangers of Overzealous Faith by Larry Osborne (Zondervan, 2012)

Confessions of a Pastor: Adventures in Dropping the Pose and Getting Real with God by Craig Groeschel (Multnomah, 2006)

Leading on Empty: Refilling Your Tank and Renewing Your Passion by Wayne Cordeiro (Bethany House, 2010)

Mad Church Disease: Overcoming the Burnout Epidemic by Anne Jackson (Zondervan, 2009)

Pastors at Greater Risk by H. B. London Jr. and Neil B. Wiseman (Regal, 2003)

Preventing Ministry Failure: A ShepherdCare Guide for Pastors, Ministers and Other Caregivers by Brad Hoffman and Michael Todd Wilson (IVP, 2007)

The Wounded Healer: Ministry in a Contemporary Society by Henri J. M. Nouwen (Image, 1979)

Grace

All Is Grace by Brennan Manning (David C. Cook, 2011)

American Grace: How Religion Divides and Unites Us by Robert D. Putnam and David E. Campbell (Simon & Schuster, 2012)

Disruptive Grace: Reflections on God, Scripture and the Church by Walter Brueggemann (Fortress, 2011)

Give Us Grace: An Anthology of Anglican Prayers by Christopher L. Webber (Morehouse, 2004)

Grace: More Than We Deserve, Greater Than We Imagine by Max Lucado (Thomas Nelson, 2012)

Grace Walk: What You've Always Wanted in the Christian Walk by Steve McVey (Harvest House, 2005)

Gracenomics: Unleash the Power of Second Chance Living by Mike Foster (People of the Second Chance, 2010)

The Great Awakening: Believing in Grace Is One Thing. Living It Is Another by Charles R. Swindoll (Thomas Nelson, 2010)

Quantum Grace: The Sunday Reading: Lenten Reflections on Creation and Connectedness by Judy Cannato (Ave Maria, 2005)

Rediscovering Daily Graces: Classic Voices on the Transforming Power of the Sacraments by Robert Elmer (NavPress, 2006)

What's So Amazing about Grace? by Philip Yancey (Zondervan, 2002)

Forgiveness

Unpacking Forgiveness: Biblical Answers for Complex Questions and Deep Wounds by Chris Brauns (Crossway, 2008)

Church Models/Practice

An Army of Ordinary People: Stories of Real-Life Men and Women Simply Being the Church by Felicity Dale (Tyndale, 2010)

Authentic Faith: The Power of a Fire-Tested Life by Gary Thomas (Zondervan, 2003)

Breaking the Missional Code: Your Church Can Become a Missionary in Your Community by Ed Stetzer and David Putman (B&H Academic, 2006)

Christianity for the Rest of Us: How the Neighborhood Church Is Transforming the Faith by Diana Butler Bass (HarperOne, 2007)

A Christianity Worth Believing: Hope-Filled, Open-Armed, Alive-and-Well Faith for the Left Out, Left Behind, and Let Down in Us All by Doug Pagitt (Jossey-Bass, 2009)

Creating a Missional Culture: Equipping the Church for the Sake of the World by JR Woodward (IVP, 2012)

Emergence Christianity: What It Is, Where It Is Going, and Why It Matters by Phyllis Tickle (Baker 2012)

The Forgotten Ways: Reactivating the Missional Church by Alan Hirsch (Brazos, 2009)

Hipster Christianity: When Church and Cool Collide by Brett McCracken (Baker, 2010)

The House Church Book: Rediscover the Dynamic, Organic, Relational, Viral Community Jesus Started by Wolfgang Simson and George Barna (BarnaBooks, 2009)

Houses That Change the World by Wolfgang Simson (Authentic, 2001)

If the Church Were Christian by Philip Gulley (HarperOne, 2011)

The Indigenous Church by Melvin L. Hodges (Gospel, 1976)

The Irresistible Revolution: Living as an Ordinary Radical by Shane Claiborne and Jim Wallis (Zondervan, 2006)

Living into Community: Cultivating Practices That Sustain Us by Christine D. Pohl (Eerdmans, 2011)

Making Room: Recovering Hospitality as a Christian Tradition by Christine D. Pohl (Eerdmans, 1999)

Missional Communities: The Rise of the Post-Congregational Church by Reggie McNeal (Jossey-Bass, 2011)

A Meal with Jesus: Discovering Grace, Community, and Mission around the Table by Tim Chester (Crossway, 2011)

Misreading Scripture through Western Eyes: Removing Cultural Blinders to Better Understand the Bible by E. Randolph Richards and Brandon J. O'Brien (IVP, 2012)

More Jesus, Less Religion: Moving from Rules to Relationship by Stephen Arterburn and Jack Felton (WaterBrook, 2010)

The Next Evangelicalism: Freeing the Church from Western Cultural Captivity by Soong-Chan Rah (IVP, 2009)

Open Source Church: Making Room for the Wisdom of All by Landon Whitsitt (The Alban Institute, 2011)

Organic Church: Growing Faith Where Life Happens by Neil Cole (Jossey-Bass, 2005)

Portable Faith: How to Take Your Church to the Community by Sarah Cunningham (Abingdon, 2013)

Red Letter Revolution: What If Jesus Really Meant What He Said? by Shane Claiborne and Tony Campolo (Thomas Nelson, 2012)

Reimagining Church: Pursuing the Dream of Organic Christianity by Frank Viola (David C. Cook, 2008)

Reluctant Pilgrim: A Moody, Somewhat Self-Indulgent Introvert's Search for Spiritual Community by Enuma Okoro (Fresh Air, 2010)

The Sacred Way: Spiritual Practices for Everyday Life by Tony Jones (Zondervan, 2005)

Simple Church: Returning to God's Process for Making Disciples by Thom S. Rainer and Eric Geiger (B&H, 2011)

The Underground Church: Reclaiming the Subversive Way of Jesus by Robin Meyers (Jossey-Bass, 2012)

What Jesus Started: Joining the Movement, Changing the World by Steve Addison (IVP, 2012)

When the Church Was a Family: Recapturing Jesus' Vision for Authentic Christian Community by Joseph H. Hellerman (B&H, 2009)

When "Spiritual but Not Religious" Is Not Enough: Seeing God in Surprising Places by Lillian Daniel (Jericho, 2013)

LINKS

Brandon Ambrosino. "Finding a Faith of Our Own." *Relevant.* http://www.relevantmagazine.com/god/god-our-generation/finding-faith-our-own

"Are You Disillusioned with Church, Feeling Let Down, Tired, Hurt, and Misunderstood?" Grow. http://growworld.org/burned-out-christians/

Dietrich Bonhoeffer. "Disillusioned with Your Church." http://www.hiswayministries.org/fddisillusion.htm

Andrew Byers. "Discipling the Disillusioned." Gospel Centered Discipleship. http://www.gospelcentereddiscipleship.com/discipling-the-disillusioned/

Camerin Courtney. "Blessed Disillusionment." *Today's Christian Woman.* http://www.todayschristianwoman.com/articles/2005 /march/mind50330.html

John D. Duncan. "Six Reasons People Leave Your Church." LifeWay Church Resources. http://www.lifeway.com/lwc/files/lwcF_PDF _Why_Members_Leave.pdf

Willmore D. Eva. "Take a Dose of Disillusionment." *Ministry.* https:// www.ministrymagazine.org/archive/1998/04/take-a-dose-of -disillusionment

Katie Galli. "Dear Disillusioned Generation." *Christianity Today.* http://www.christianitytoday.com/ct/2008/april/28.69.html

Hedgehog. "A 'Church' for the Disillusioned and Other Questions on Doubt." Wheat and Tares. http://www.wheatandtares.org/12488/a -church-for-the-disillusioned-and-other-questions-on-doubt/

Alan Jaimieson. "Ten Myths about Church Leavers." Battered Sheep. http://www.batteredsheep.com/myths.html

David Kinnaman. "Six Reasons Young Christians Leave Church." Barna Group. https://www.barna.org/teens-next-gen-articles/528-six-reasons -young-christians-leave-church

Joel J. Miller. "Disillusioned by the Church." Patheos. http://www. patheos.com/blogs/joeljmiller/2013/04/disillusioned-by-the-church/

Mark Naylor. "Disillusioned with the Sunday Expression of Church." Northwest Baptist Seminary. http://www.nbseminary.ca/archives/ disillusioned-with-the-sunday-meeting-expression-of-church

Barb Orlowski. "From Trust to Dust." Church Exiters. http://www. churchexiters.com/2012/12/from-trust-to-dust/

Glenn Packiam. "Why We Must Get Disillusioned with 'Community.'" ChurchLeaders.Com. http://www.churchleaders.com/worship/worship -blogs/161061-glenn_packiam_why_we_must_get_disillusioned_with _community.html

Becky Pamer. "How to Survive Church." Beliefnet. http://www.beliefnet
.com/Faiths/Christianity/2006/01/How-To-Survive-Church.aspx

Philip Yancey. "Faith and Doubt." PhilipYancey.com. http://www
.philipyancey.com/q-and-a-topics/faith-and-doubt

SONGS

All the Poor and Powerless

Amazing Grace

Amazing Love

Beautiful Day

Beautiful Things

Bless the Lord — Ten Thousand Reasons

Blessed Assurance

Blessed Be the Name of the Lord

Blessed Be Your Name

Bones

Brokenness Aside

Come by Here

Come to Me

Cornerstone

Create in Me a Clean Heart

Day after Day

Desert Song

Everything Falls

Fail Us Not

He Is with You

He Will Carry Me

He's Always Been Faithful

His Eye Is on the Sparrow

Hold Me, Jesus

How Firm a Foundation

How Great Thou Art

I Need Thee Every Hour

I Will Rise

In the Garden

Into the Darkness

It Is Well with My Soul

Jesus, Lover of My Soul

Lead Me to the Cross

Love Song

My Mind Played a Trick on Me

My Redeemer Lives

Never Alone

Never Once

One Thing Remains

Our God

Our God Saves

Overcomer

Praise You in the Storm

Precious Lord

Redeemed

Rock of Ages

Strong to Rescue

Stronger
Take My Hand
Thank You for Saving Me
There Is a Fountain
'Tis So Sweet to Trust in
  Jesus
What a Day That Will Be
What a Friend We Have in
  Jesus

When the Tears Fall
Where Feet May Fail
Whom Shall I Fear?
Yearn
You Are Mine
You Invite Me In
You Make Beautiful Things
You Never Let Go
Your Love Never Fails

SCRIPTURES

Certainly the Bible serves us best when taken in context and when considering how each text would have been received by the people it was written for. Understanding then that these verses are most accurately understood in their larger context, the following passages are suggestive of hope for believers. And while they can't be used as magical prayers borrowed from ancient people, they can be encouraging because they tell us something about the nature of God and the goodwill and hope he inspires in humans in their hardest moments.

Deuteronomy 7:9
Deuteronomy 31:6
Joshua 1:9
Psalm 1:1 – 3
Psalm 9:9 – 10
Psalm 16:8
Psalm 18:32 – 36
Psalm 23
Psalm 27:1
Psalm 34:17 – 19
Psalm 36:3 – 6

Psalm 37:1
Psalm 37:4 – 5
Psalm 46:1 – 3
Psalm 51:10
Psalm 55:22
Psalm 118:8
Psalm 119:9 – 11
Proverbs 1:7
Proverbs 3:5 – 6
Proverbs 24:14
Proverbs 30:5

Ecclesiastes 3:1
Ecclesiastes 3:14
Isaiah 40:30 – 31
Isaiah 41:10
Isaiah 43:18 – 19
Isaiah 53:5
Isaiah 54:17
Isaiah 55:11
Jeremiah 17:7 – 8
Jeremiah 32:27
Jeremiah 33:3
Nahum 1:7
Zephaniah 3:17
Matthew 5:8
Matthew 6:25 – 27
Matthew 7:2
Matthew 11:28 – 30
John 1:12
John 8:32
John 14:1 – 3
John 14:27
John 15:4 – 5
John 16:33
Acts 2:38
Romans 5:2 – 5
Romans 8:1

Romans 8:28
Romans 8:38 – 39
Romans 12:1 – 2
Romans 12:12 – 14
1 Corinthians 4:5
1 Corinthians 4:16 – 18
1 Corinthians 10:13
1 Corinthians 13:13
1 Corinthians 15:57 – 58
2 Corinthians 4:8 – 9
2 Corinthians 4:16 – 18
Galatians 5:22 – 26
Galatians 6:9
Philippians 1:6
Philippians 3:7 – 8
Philippians 3:13
Philippians 4:4 – 8
Philippians 4:13
1 Thessalonians 5:18
2 Timothy 1:7
1 Peter 5:6 – 7
Hebrews 11:1
James 1:2 – 4
James 1:12
1 John 5:14

Acknowledgments

Special thanks to my parents,
Harold and Elizabeth Raymond,
who led the first Christian community I ever belonged to:
my family.

My brothers, David and John,
who model the love of spiritual siblings while
tormenting me like genetic ones.

My coconspirators, Jennie and Bethany,
who continue to believe we can change the world.
The people of Cornerstone, Westwinds, and Rivertree,
who helped me fall in love and stay in love with the local church,

and

many church leaders I've met across the religious landscape
who continually inspire me to love the global one.
And most of all, my husband, Chuck, and my children —
Justus and Malachi —
who partner with me in living and being church
to our local world.
I am grateful to Jesus, the head of the church,
for teaming me with people like these.

Notes

1. Sarah Cunningham, *Portable Faith: How to Take Your Church to the Community* (Nashville: Abingdon, 2013), 8.
2. Sarah Cunningham, *Picking Dandelions: A Search for Eden among Life's Weeds* (Grand Rapids: Zondervan, 2010), 42.
3. Rebecca Barnes and Linda Lowry, "7 Startling Facts: An Up-Close Look at Church Attendance in America," ChurchLeaders.Com, http://www.churchleaders.com /pastors/pastor-articles/139575-7-startling-facts-an-up-close-look-at-church -attendance-in-america.html (accessed November 19, 2013).
4. "What People Experience in Churches," The Barna Group, January 9, 2012: https://www.barna.org/ congregations-articles/556-what-people-experience-in-churches.
5. "Experiences of Protestant Ministers Who Left Local Church Ministry," *Pulpit and Pew*, October 25, 2003, http://pulpitandpew.org/sites/all/themes/pulpitandpew /files/Hoge.pdf.
6. Lillian Daniel, "When Spiritual but Not Religious Is Not Enough: Seeing God in Unexpected Places, Even the Church," Jericho Books, http://jerichobooks.com /portfolio/when-spiritual-but-not-religious-is-not-enough/.
7. Andy Stanley, *Visioneering* (Sisters, OR: Multnomah, 1999), 17.
8. N. T. Wright, *The Challenge of Jesus* (Downers Grove, IL: InterVarsity, 1999), 31.
9. Richard Foster, *Prayer: Finding the Heart's True Home* (New York: Harper Collins, 1964), 7–8.
10. Tim Stafford, "The Church — Why Bother?" *Christianity Today*, January 2005, 44.
11. Center for the Study of Global Christianity (2011), http://www.pewforum.org /uploadedFiles/Topics/Religious_Affiliation/Christian/ChristianityAppendixB .pdf.
12. List taken from Cunningham, *Portable Faith*, 96.
13. http://pastorjonathanmartin.com/renovatus/defining-experience-of–2010–4 -becoming-our-grandmothers-church-with-geoffrey-wainwright-rickie-moore-and -jacqui-smith/.

14. Rev. Lillian Daniel on "Spiritual but Not Religious," *Religion and Ethics Newsweekly*, http://video.pbs.org/video/2328958695/.

15. "Theodore Roosevelt Association," *Man in the Arena*: www.theodoreroosevelt.org /life/quotes.htm.

16. Bill Hybels, *Courageous Leadership: Field-Tested Strategy for the 360-Degree Leader* (Grand Rapids: Zondervan, 2012), 35.

17. Sarah Cunningham, *The Well-Balanced World Changer: A Field Guide for Staying Sane While Doing Good* (Chicago: Moody, 2013).

18. Neil Howe and William Strauss, *Millennials Rising: The Next Generation* (New York: Vintage, 2000), 4.

19. Robert E. Webber, *The Younger Evangelicals* (Grand Rapids: Baker, 2002), 157.

20. Peg Tyre, "Bringing Up Adultolescents," *Newsweek*, March 25 2002, 34.

21. Thom Rainer, quoted in Rob Phillipson, "Research: American 'Millennials' Value Family above All Else," LifeWay, http://www.lifeway.com/Article/LifeWay-Research -finds-American-Millennials-value-family-above-all-else.

22. "Millennials: Confident. Connected. Open to Change," Pew Research Social and Demographic Trends, http://www.pewsocialtrends.org/2010/02/24/ millennials-confident-connected-open-to-change/.

23. "Beyond Red vs. Blue: The Political Typology," Pew Charitable Trusts, May 4, 2011: http://www.pewtrusts.org/our_work_report_detail.aspx?id=85899359459.

24. Jeffrey Jensen Arnett, " 'The Empathic Civilization': The Young Pioneers of the Empathic Generation," Huff Post Books, The Blog, http://www.huffingtonpost. com/jeffrey-jensen-arnett/the-empathic-civilization_b_454211.html; Eric H. Greenberg and Karl Weber, *Generation We: How Millennial Youth Are Taking Over America and Changing Our World Forever* (Emeryville, CA: Pachatusan, 2008); Catherine Rampell, "A Generation of Slackers? Not So Much," *New York Times*, May 28, 2011, http://www.nytimes.com/2011/05/29/weekinreview/29graduates .html; Howe and Strauss, *Millennials Rising*; Morley Winograd and Michael D. Hais, *Millennial Momentum: How a New Generation Is Remaking America* (Piscataway, NJ: Rutgers University Press, 2011).

25. Gerald Schlabach, *And Who Is My Neighbor?* (Scottdale, PA: Herald, 1990), 17.

26. Joseph Heath and Andrew Potter, *Nation of Rebels: Why Counterculture Became Consumer Culture* (New York: Harper Business), 100.

27. "Young, Underemployed, and Optimistic," Pew Research Social and Demographic Trends, February 9, 2012: http://www.pewsocialtrends.org/2012/02/09/young -underemployed-and-optimistic/.

28. Raphael Snir and Itzhak Harpaz, "Beyond Workaholism: Towards a General Model of Heavy Work Investment," *Elselvier Human Resource Management Review*, https:// www.mta.ac.il/December/Beyond_Workaholism.pdf.

29. Chris Michalak, "What Employees Really Want," Towers Perrin: http://www.towersperrin.com/tp/getwebcachedoc?webc=TILL/USA /2002/200203/2002041805.pdf.

30. Eric Chester, *Employing Generation Why* (Lakewood, CO: Tucker, 2002), 13.

31. Christopher Muther, "The Growing Culture of Impatience Makes Us Crave More and More Instant Gratification," Boston.com, http://www.boston.com/lifestyle /specials/2013/02/01/the-growing-culture-impatience-where-instant-gratification -makes-crave-more-instant-gratification/eu5SPWCVTmFp9Nm6dUndhP/story .html.

32. Ibid.

33. Dana Levin, quoted in Janna Anderson and Lee Rainie, "Millennials Will Benefit and Suffer Due to Their Hyperconnected Lives," Pew Internet, February 29, 2012, http://pewinternet.org/Reports/2012/Hyperconnected-lives/Main-findings /Negative-effects.aspx.

34. Pew Research Center's Internet & American Life Project, cited in Christopher Muther, "Instant Gratification Is Making Us Perpetually Impatient," *Boston Globe*, February 2, 2013, http://www.bostonglobe.com/lifestyle/style/2013/02/01/the -growing-culture-impatience-where-instant-gratification-makes-crave-more -instant-gratification/q8tWDNGeJB2mm45fQxtTQP/story.html.

35. "Next-Generation Strategies for Advertising to Millennials," http://www.comscore .com/Insights/Presentations_and_Whitepapers/2012/Next_Generation_Strategies _for_Advertising_to_Millennials.

36. John R. Quain, "Why Today's High-Tech Cars Can Drive You Crazy," FoxNews. com, August 28, 2013, http://www.foxnews.com/tech/2013/08/28/why-today -high-tech-cars-can-drive-crazy/.

37. Joanne Chen, "Is Your High-Tech Life Making You Sick?" *Marie Claire*, July 22, 2011, http://www.marieclaire.com/health-fitness/advice/tech-scares#slide-1.

38. Jennifer LeClaire, "Kids and Tech: How Much Is Too Much?" *TechNewsWorld*, September 6, 2006, http://www.technewsworld.com/story/52677.html.

39. CBS / *New York Times* poll cited in Susan Dominus, "The Mysterious Disappear- ance of Young Pro-Choice Women," *Glamour*, August 2005, Vol. 103 Issue 8, 200.

40. Dominus, "Mysterious Disappearance of Young Pro-Choice Women," 200.

41. Stephanie Simon, "Youth Movement against Abortion," *Seattle Times*, originally published in *Los Angeles Times* on January 23, 2008, http://seattletimes.com/html /nationworld/2004139782_abortionyouths23.html.

42. "Grand Old Party for a Brand New Generation," http://images.skem1.com/client _id_32089/Grand_Old_Party_for_a_Brand_New_Generation.pdf, 60–61.

43. http://www.amazon.com/Delaying-Real-World-Twentysomethings-Adventure /dp/B000AEFEL6.

44. Colleen Kinder, quoted in ibid.

45. Frank F. Furstenberg, quoted in Patricia Cohen, "Long Road to Adulthood Is Growing Even Longer," *New York Times*, June 12, 2010, http://www.nytimes.com /2010/06/13/us/13generations.html.

46. Clark University Poll, http://www.clarku.edu/clarkpoll/.

47. Randall S. Hansen, Ph.D, "Navigating the Quarterlife Crisis to Career and Personal Success: Five Strategies for Fulfilling Your Dreams," QuintCareers, http://www .quintcareers.com/quarterlife_career_crisis.html (accessed November 17, 2013).

48. Quoted in Jeanne Meister, "Three Reasons You Need to Adopt a Millenial Mindset Regardless of Your Age," *Forbes*: http://www.forbes.com/sites/jeannemeister /2012/10/05/millennialmindse/ (accessed November 17, 2013).

49. Craig Dunham, "Motivating Twentysomethings. They're Here. Now What?" *Group's Church Volunteer Central*: http://www.churchvolunteercentral.com/7251 /motivating-twentysomethings-theyre-here-now-what/ (July, 2005).

50. Quoted in Patricia Kirk, "Developers Give Gen Y What They Want," *Urbanland*: http://urbanland.uli.org/industry-sectors/residential/developers-give-gen-y-what -they-want/ (June 1, 2011).

51. Dan Reed, "More Homebuyers Want Walkable, Transit-Served Communities," Greater Greater Washington, August 18, 2011, http://greatergreaterwashington.org /post/11722/more-homebuyers-want-walkable-transit-served-communities/.

52. http://urbanland.uli.org/Articles/2011/June/KirkEcho.

53. Donald Appleyard, *Livable Streets* (Berkeley, CA: University of California Press, 1981).

54. "Gen Y Shoppers, Raised on E-Commerce, Still Prefer In-Store Experience," Lorraine Mirabella, *Baltimore Sun*, September 7, 2013, http://articles.baltimoresun.com /2013_09_07/business/bs-bz-gen-y-shoppers_20130907_1_shopping-center -millennials-gen-y.

55. Kimberly Weisul, "Consumers Buy Into 'Buy Local,'" *Bloomberg Businessweek*, February 18, 2010, http://www.businessweek.com/magazine/content/10_09 /b4168057813351.htm.

56. Ibid.

57. Denver Urban Gardens, "Growing Community Gardens," http://dug.org/storage /public-documents/DUG_Best_Practices_digital_copy.pdf.

58. Ann Byle, "Community Gardens," *Grand Rapids Magazine*, http://www.grmag.com /features/09-09/09-09.htm.

59. Portland Parks & Recreation, "Healthy Parks, Healthy Portland," Community Gardens Business Plan, May 2009, http://www.portlandoregon.gov/parks/article /246846.

60. Boston Natural Areas Network, "Boston Is Growing Gardens (BIGG) Dorchester," http://www.bostonnatural.org/cgBIGG.htm.

61. "Community Gardens Growing at Record Pace across the City," City of Vancouver, June 6, 2012, http://vancouver.ca/news-calendar/community-gardens-growing-at-record-pace-across-the-city.aspx.

62. Sarah Cunningham, *Portable Faith: How to Take Your Church to the Community* (Nashville: Abingdon, 2013).

63. Eric Chester, *Employing Generation Why* (Lakewood, CO: Tucker House, 2002), 13.

64. Holly Hall, "Half of American Teenagers Volunteer, Largely Because Their Friends Do," *Chronicle of Philanthropy*, October 24, 2012, http://philanthropy.com/article/Half-of-American-Teenagers/135278/.

65. "Study Suggests Young People Are Delaying Marriage Because of Rising College Debt," *Huff Post*, October 9, 2013, http://www.huffingtonpost.com/2012/03/28/study-college-debt-marriage-loans-rates-rising_n_1385548.html.

66. "Waiting, Waiting, Waiting: First-Time Parents Getting Older," LifeSiteNews.com, January 25, 2013, http://www.lifesitenews.com/news/waiting-waiting-waiting-first-time-parents-getting-older/.

67. Steve Finlay, "Why Toyota Wants Gen Y," *Keep Media*: www.keepmedia.com/pubs/WardsDealerBusiness/ (January 1, 2003).

68. Quoted in "Generation Y Goes Shopping," *Chief Marketer*: http://www.chiefmarketer.com/database-marketing/generation-y-is-goes-shopping-14072005 (accessed November 17, 2013).

69. http://www.census.gov/prod/cen2010/briefs/c2010br-02.pdf.

70. Sabrina Tavernise, "Whites Account for Under Half of Births in U.S." *New York Times*, May 17, 2012, http://www.nytimes.com/2012/05/17/us/whites-account-for-under-half-of-births-in-us.html?pagewanted=all&_r=0.

71. http://www.childstats.gov/americaschildren/famsoc1.asp.

72. http://www.census.gov/prod/2012pubs/p70-131.pdf.

73. http://www.census.gov/prod/2013pubs/acs-22.pdf.

74. http://www.census.gov/compendia/statab/2012/tables/12s0229.pdf.

75. http://www.census.gov/compendia/statab/2012/tables/12s0696.xls.

76. Marilyn Brenden, "Ministering to Missing Class Members," *The Clergy Journal*: http://connection.ebscohost.com/c/articles/8869855/ministering-missing-class-members (accessed November 17, 2013).

77. Michael Emerson, *People of the Dream: Multi-Racial Congregations in the United States* (Princeton, NJ: Princeton University Press, 2006), 39.

78. Tom Huang, "The Diversity Gap," Poynter Online, June 16, 2003, www.poynter.org/column.asp?id=58&aid=37934.

79. Linda Kulman, "Betty Ford: A First Lady Who Always Tells It Like It Is," *U.S. News and World Report*, August 2001, 68.

80. Ibid.

81. Sam Vincent Meddis, "The Web's Unexpected Political Clout," *USA Today*: www.usatoday.com/tech/columnist/ccb0914.htm (September 14, 1998).

82. Ibid.

83. "Talk Shows," *The Museum of Broadcast Communications*: http://www.museum.tv/eotv/talkshows.htm (accessed November 17, 2013).

84. "Jerry Springer," *Wikipedia*: en.wikipedia.org/wiki/Jerry_Springer (accessed November 17, 2013).